Who Are They Going To Believe?

BY
RAY C. DUFFY

BASED ON A TRUE STORY

"Dedicated to those who have been, and still are being screwed by a broken system. Never give up! It will all be worth it in the long run." – Ray C. Duffy

"To the man who told me his story and let me share it with the world...You no longer have to keep this pain that you've been hiding to yourself. Today and from here on out, you now stand in front of the shadows. Your voice matters!" - Ray C. Duffy

Based on a true story…

Who Are They Going To Believe?

"Warning: this book occasionally contains strong language (which may be unsuitable for children), unusual humor (which may be unsuitable for adults), and things that may be inappropriate for my mother to read. (I'm sorry in advance mom. Love you!)."

Contents

CHAPTER 1

TIME

Zrrr...Zrrr...Zrrr...

My phone vibrated, and it jolted me to rise from my sleep. I saw notifications pop up on my phone like crazy. It was 5:15 AM and a Saturday morning. Awakened, I sat on my bed and touched my ruffled hair with my eyes half-closed. The thought of not being in bed till 8:00 AM, just as I had planned, made me upset. I wondered, "Who could have interrupted my rest?" I sat still and my phone continued chiming, alerting me that I had notifications. It took me a second to gain focus but when I did, I saw a blonde woman by the name of Lucy, liking a mass number of my pictures as though her entire life depended on it. I could have decided to not pay attention to this, but I had to because it woke me up. It made me question, what was behind the reason for the early morning surprise, thrown off by a stranger I knew nothing about. I wondered if this stranger had no shame in liking a multiple amount of my pictures just to be noticed. Perhaps, she was someone I had met before. After a while, I realized I couldn't recall where I had met her, and I was certain I had never seen her before. I turned my phone off, placed it down, and went back to bed. I still felt sleepy, and my eyes were weak. So, I closed them gently.

A few minutes later, I was on my feet because I couldn't sleep any longer. I realized, staying in bed until 8:00 AM was a bad idea anyway. I made coffee and stood by the window-side adoring nature. The chirping of fluttering birds, on bending branches, fascinated me. I said to myself,

"Today, I am going to be like a bird...Rise in the morning, sing, and get things done." Moments later, a cool gust of wind brushed my face and whipped me back into reality. I was set to sort out tasks this weekend since I was home.

"The gym, sauna, hike, meditate, grocery shop, meal prep, clean, attend a few meetings, spend time with friends and family..." I muttered, listing my plans for the day.

I had forgotten about the stranger for a while, until I realized she liked ten more of my pictures at a time. She would stop for a while and then repeat this process randomly. It was obvious she was trying to get my attention. I continued with my tasks and planned more on how to spend the rest of my week.

One week, two weeks, three weeks…This stalking continued, and this stranger had no plan to stop liking my pictures. I figured, I needed to do something. So, I clicked on her profile to see what she was about.

"I still don't think we've met." I said and scrolled through her profile. I accidently double tapped by clicking twice on one of her pictures. She liked three of my pictures right back, to let me know she was aware that I was checking out her profile. I did not want to make this situation look awkward, so I messaged her on Facebook, "Hey, how are you?"

Lucy replied immediately and we began to exchange small talk back and forth. It started with questions pertaining to our favorite things we both love to do, favorite types of food, favorite sports, favorite colors and more. After a few weeks, I asked her if she would like to hang out with me and she said, "Of course." She sent me her address and I drove to her house. I arrived and met her dressed up and ready. She was putting on a white cardigan, over her plain tee shirt, wore light blue jeans, "hippy like" sandals, and had on light makeup.

"It's so nice to finally hang out with you." She said with excitement, as I stood by the door with my hands rested in my pockets.

"Same here." I watched her grab her purse and close the door. She giggled and walked to my car. As a gentleman, I opened the door for her, started the car and drove off.

"So, where are we grabbing drinks?" She asked.

"How about The Compass?" I replied. She smirked back as if she was trying to hide the disappointment. She kept mute for a while and blurted out that there was a different place she had in mind close by. I cruised past a few buildings and pedestrians near the beach. She asked me to turn left, and I did. She pointed at a bar, and said, "That's the place. Cantina's! Let's go there." I searched for parking, found a spot, parked, and then we both went in. Greeted by the bartender, we requested a bottle of wine and drank a few glasses. Silence overshadowed our space in the bar and we both sat in silence. I tried starting a conversation, but our conversation was dry, and I learned I didn't like her as much as I thought I would. I decided I wouldn't kiss her on our "first date" since I was less attracted to her during that moment. I was a little turned off by her vibes because I did not feel any type of connection. On the way to her house, we barely spoke until we approached her neighborhood.

"Well, this is my street coming up." Lucy said.

"Right on!" I said with some excitement because I was finally relieved that the "date" was over. I parked in front of her apartment, looked at her, and she stepped out of my car slowly. I felt like I was being a dick because I kept the car running as I sat in my seat staring at her. So instead, I got out and walked her to the door.

"See you again?" She said, flashing a shy smile at me while she stood, cross-legged at her door.

"Goodnight." I muttered, gave her a fake smile, and hugged her coldly, making sure there was a space between us even while we hugged. I drove off after this awkward moment and watched her close the door.

"I had such a great time with you, and I cannot wait to do it again." 30 minutes later, I read Lucy's message. I made it home safely and began demolishing homemade tacos, which I had in my fridge from the night before. I munched on them and almost choked when I saw this message. It made me cringe. I read her message and did not reply. I was afraid that I could be stuck in a situation I would not like in the near future. The next day, I woke up to seeing Lucy liking three of my pictures and a good morning text. During that time, I worked for the city, and my schedule was nice, the work was not so demanding, and this led me to having an open block on most days. Bored and tired of doing things alone, I decided to hang out with Lucy again. We ended up going on more "dates." And then, some more "dates..." The more we hung out, the more drinks I watched her order and finish in one sitting. Lucy would always demand to eat at high-end restaurants. She would order the most expensive dish on the menu, never finish it, order a few more random things, pick at them, and then slide the bill over to me every time. This made me shocked, but I preferred to play the role of a nice and cool gentleman.

On one of our "dates," we ate at a cool restaurant that I never knew existed. We sat on opposite ends from each other, listened to live music, and embraced the delightful vibes of the environment.

"Welcome. What would you guys like to order?" The waiter asked, standing with a large notepad clutched between his fingers.

"The vegetarian bowl, mozzarella sticks, oysters, the cheese platter, fries, coconut rice and calamari." Lucy requested, as she went through the menu.

"And for you sir?" The waiter asked.

"I will just take a water, beer, and fries." I replied. I wanted to keep it light because I was more interested in Lucy. "Who was this little blonde woman from Oceanside?" I thought to myself. When our food came, Lucy barely ate any of it and ordered more drinks instead. When the waiter gave us the bill, she slid it over to me once again.

"You got this right?" She said.

"Yeah…" I said as I pulled out my debit card without checking the bill. I placed it on top of the black folder and smiled at Lucy.

"So…Do you go out often?" I asked. Lucy looked at me and chugged her drinks. "Nope…Well, sometimes." She said. Lucy started to open up about her childhood and tell me stories about random things. I was intrigued. After that moment, I began to become attracted to her weirdness. It made me eager to find out who she truly was. "Why the heck was I so interested in this woman?" I said to myself.

One night, after another "date," we went out for a few drinks. I usually don't drink hard liquor but that night I did. I had three tall glasses of Jack and coke. When we got back to her house, the liquor finally settled in. She stood at her door and went on about how great her night was with me. She also talked about how Poseidon's restaurant's food tasted better than Pacifica Del Mar's. As she chatted, she kept coming closer to me. She pulled me into herself as if she wanted to smash our souls together. I was unable to resist the urge to kiss her due to the liquor playing with my emotions. So, I went along with it.

"Would you like to stay the night?" Lucy questioned as she invited me in, clutching my hands in hers.

"Sure..." I replied and went in. I sat on the couch, and she said, "I will be right back." Lucy went upstairs and changed into some comfy clothes. She went into her kitchen, poured two glasses of wine, gave me a glass, and then sat next to me. We watched Netflix for a few hours until we began to get tired.

"Do you know Luigi?" She asked.

"Luigi?" I said with confusion.

"Yeah! Luigi Rojales. He has slick brown hair, he is about your height, he has a bunch of tattoos, went to school with us, and I think he is about to join the Navy. He stayed here once. He slept in my bed and everything. We didn't do much but yeah…"

12

Lucy said.

"Oh yeah. I do know him. But hey, I am tired. And I think I am sober enough to drive home." I said. "Why did she bring up Luigi? Was she trying to make me jealous?" I asked myself.

"No, you should stay the night. I wouldn't want you to get pulled over." Lucy said.

"Ok. I am down." I said. And then Lucy and I went up to her bedroom. I took off my shirt and pants and climbed into her bed. Lucy turned off the lights and put her legs and feet on me. She kept touching my chest, teasing me, and then said, "We are not doing anything just to let you know." I said, "I was only planning on sleeping." And plus, I was already turned off by her talking about Luigi. She continued to touch me and slide her foot up and down my leg. This went on for a few moments and then I ended up falling asleep. The next morning, I left early because I had to be up for work, and I was a believer in the motto, "Punctuality is the soul of business." I decided to send her a message and she requested that we have the usual, "date-night" again. She suggested we go to another high-end restaurant, but I told her I was busy. I said this because I wasn't, "feeling her." Yet, she insisted that we go out. I gave in, and after dinner, she wanted me to spend the night. I told her I had to be up early and ended up going home. After that, we stopped talking for a few weeks. I refused to text her, and my life was going well just as it was before she stepped in. I was thinking about time. Time was important to me, and I was not willing to spend it in a wasteful manner. I snapped out of my curiosity for her for a moment because I could not visualize us being together in the future. In fact, I recently got out of a relationship and Lucy reminded me of why I dislike the dating scene. There were many red flags raised but that night, her spell she had me under finally broke. That night, I was ready to quit, to let go, and stop wasting money, conversations, sleep, and time over someone who was not worthy.

CHAPTER 2

THE ROAD TRIP

Today, May 2017, I received
a call from the United States Navy and was
put on active orders. I was directed to go to
New York which will be my new duty
station and was to report on June 21st, 2017.
I was excited to move to the East Coast and
start a new adventure. I loved going on trips
whether it involved work or not. I decided to
go to a location off Tamarack in Carlsbad, to
enjoy a nice solo day on the beach. This was
my hidden getaway spot. I took my shoes
off, went into the sand, and headed towards
my, "Secret location." I scrolled to my

Snapchat app on my phone, took a picture of the water, then added it to my story. I said to myself, "There's nothing more relaxing than feeling that California ocean breeze and being the only one on the beach." The calm waves and soft warm sand made me forget about every worry in the world. The gentle sound of the sea and seagulls hooting was my companion. I was savoring this wonderful moment for what it was. After, I laid down under my umbrella for a bit. I began to munch on a few snacks after realizing I could not just stand and feel nature with my stomach being empty. My gaze shifted towards a squirrel scrambling past the stones near the water and headed my way. I threw it a Cheez-It. The squirrel stopped in its tracks, looked up and began dashing towards the Cheez-It. It did not seem to be frightened of my presence. I decided we could both share the pack of Cheez-It's together and I started feeding it bit by bit. I could see the squirrel's excitement as it leaped to catch another Cheez-It with its mouth. I watched it chomp down quickly and stood still for more.

"Hey!" I heard a woman's dull voice behind me and looked back. I was stunned when I saw who it was. Lucy…She glared at me with her blue eyes. She had on a light pink buttoned up shirt, faded jeans, and carried her tan sandals in her right hand. I was confused because I was not expecting her. I was quite sure this was not a coincidence. To make the situation look less awkward, I acted as if I was excited to see her. I stood up, smiled, took my sunglasses off, and waved at her awkwardly. She continued to walk towards me and when she reached the edge of my towel, she paused and stared in silence.

"What are you doing?" She asked.

"Chillin. And you?" I replied. Lucy looked at the water and then decided to sit on my towel. I stood there for a moment, and then joined her. For now, I could not comprehend her reactions towards my short response. I did not know if she was extremely angry or disappointed. So, I was trying to be careful with my words. The last thing that I wanted to do was leave California with any type of tension. I wondered if I should tell her about how I valued time, how I felt about her, and the relationship she was trying to force is not a possibility. After a moment of silence, I coughed.

"So, why haven't you hit me up in a while?" She asked.

"I was too busy feeding squirrels Cheez-Its." I said and fake-laughed. Lucy did not think my joke was funny and kept staring at me.

I asked her, "Did you just happen to be in the area or something?"

She ignored my question and was silent instead.

"Ok then...So how's your day going?" I asked.

Still ignoring every question, she said, "I am hungry. Let's go eat. Or do you have other plans after you leave the beach?"

I looked at her and said, "Honestly...I just got here, and I don't have any plans after this. But I am a bit hungry. Let's eat!"

I only decided to go because I was tired of the awkward silence and spending time with her alone. We decided to go to a place called

"Pizza Port" in Carlsbad, California. We grabbed a few beers and ordered a pizza. It was a freshly sliced pepperoni, black olives, and mushroom pizza with a side of ranch. When the food arrived, I served Lucy a slice and dug in after. Lucy picked everything off and just ate the bread. I did not care about what she was doing because I was in my zone and enjoying every bite. After I finished my slice, I took a sip of my beer and asked, "So, how did you find me?"

"I saw your location on your Snapchat story. Duh." Lucy said. I shrugged my shoulders, took another sip of my beer, and acted as if it was not a problem. "I never really had anyone track me down like this before. Well, that I know of." I thought to myself. After lunch, we headed back to her place, and I told her I was moving to the east coast. She asked me, "How will I be getting there? Flying or driving?" And I told her, I will be driving.

She immediately said, "I'll be going with you." I told her that I will be leaving on a work trip that will last a few years. And I wouldn't mind her visiting from time to time. Even though I mentioned this, it went through one ear and out the other.

"Wait, you're going on vacation and doing a cross country road trip?" She asked. "I will be leaving on a work trip that will last a few years..." I repeated. I watched her as she stared speechless.

"That's cool. Well, I can at least drive across the United States with you."

I thought about it for a second and then said, "You know, that's not a bad idea. Having company on a long drive will make it worthwhile and less dreary." She smiled. I could sense a feeling of ecstasy in her as she looked at me. After some time, we watched Netflix and then I left after an hour.

A month went by and at 3:30 AM on a Tuesday morning, I picked her up after having a short conversation with her on the phone. She was standing outside with a brown duffel bag, and a bottle of water, clutched between her right fingers. The first stop, we decided to head to Tucson Arizona to see my brother. Lucy and I spent the night at his place and had a great time. My brother made us fish, rice, and veggies for dinner. It tasted like heaven because he cooked for a living. He graduated from the Arts Institute with a culinary arts degree. We each shared embarrassing stories of our lives and Lucy got to know us on a different level. We joked and laughed as we tried taking turns talking. Everyone had something to say that was filled with non-stop laughter. We watched a few movies and ended up passing out on the couch. After that night, I began to have some feelings for Lucy. The change in her personality showed me a completely different side of her. And I liked it.

For the next stop, we stayed at her cousin's house in Phoenix Arizona. We had a great time with them and enjoyed every moment. Throughout most of the drive, Lucy was kind, and we had interesting conversations. The awkwardness I once experienced with her did not exist. I learned; she was just a girl who wanted to take a trip across the country for the first time. This was not the same Lucy who would stalk a guy and like a whole bunch of his pictures for attention, drink like a pirate, and create multiple awkward moments just because she wanted to. I felt like she had my back throughout the trip and just wanted to make my life easier. I got pulled over a total of nine times. And every time the cops saw Lucy, they asked her if she was with me, and she would say "Yes." The cops wouldn't pay any attention to me. They would smile at Lucy and say, "Bye now! And be safe."

Lucy looked at me and said, "So I guess this is what it's like to be black." She laughed. I usually laugh at a lot of things, but this joke didn't tickle my fancy. In fact, it made me feel uncomfortable for a moment. Yet again, I felt mixed emotions about Lucy just when things were going so well. But I brushed it off.

When we finally made it to New York, we spent the night in a haunted hotel, and then I dropped her off at the airport the next day.

As Lucy shut my car door. I rolled the windows down because she looked like she was going to say something important. "See you soon!" Lucy said. "See you soon?" I said impassively, as I scratched my head.

"Yeah…SEE YOU SOON…" Lucy shouted.

"Ok…Have a great flight and let me know when you make it home safely." I said, forcing a smile. Two weeks went by, and we stayed in contact. I was beginning to see her as a cool person, a good buddy that was in the friend zone. I was not ready for a relationship. Especially with her.

Beep…Beep…Beep…
I looked at my phone and Lucy was calling. I picked up.

"Hey what's up?" I asked.

"I want to see you next week. Is it ok if I stay for a little?" Lucy Asked.

"I will be working most of the time but if

you don't mind that, then sure. You are more than welcome to visit." I replied. Lucy agreed and said, "I am booking my ticket tonight."

CHAPTER 3

HAPPY BIRTHDAY TO ME...
JUST KIDDDING

A week later, I picked up Lucy from
the airport. She had a great amount of
luggage with her, and I was happy to see
another person from my hometown on the
east coast. We spent a couple of days
together and we had a lot of fun. I realized,
I've seen different sides of her, different
actions, and different mannerisms. While we
were having dinner, my phone beeped
because I was receiving notifications on my
latest post. It was a picture of me with a
caption describing New York. Immediately
and with great effort, Lucy snatched my
phone.

"Listen to me, I don't like it when girls contact you. You are with me now and I am your priority." She said. I laughed because I thought she was joking. But when I looked at her facial expression, it indicated that she meant it. She scowled and grumbled.

"I didn't fly across the U.S. just to be your buddy. I'm worth more than that! I packed up my stuff, closed out my apartment, and quit my job just to be with you. And I won't tolerate you speaking to other women while I am around." She rattled.

I looked at her confusingly and said, "I seriously thought you were joking." I stared at her, still trying to figure out if she was playing with me or not. She gulped the rest of the red wine which we had both poured earlier. I finished up my wine as well and kept staring in dismay. Before I could continue speaking, she started cursing and gazed wickedly at me. Lucy acted like a possessed group of demons that were shouting while eating flesh off their rivals back. When she began to settle down, I told her that it was fine if she wanted to stay for a bit longer. I said this because I knew I'd barely see her. My job scheduled me to fly out of town for the next few months. The fun that we were having for the first few days, diminished, and faded immediately. The atmosphere was tense. And I felt the friction between us. Lucy's attitude changed towards me. I also noticed that she started checking my phone constantly, as if we were an insecure couple. Over time, she would glare at me like Freddy Krueger and try to fight me for no reason. That is when I realized, she could not bear to see me active on any social media platform. She became impetuous, over-anxious, and always curious to know what I was doing. She treated me like I was her slave that must please her every moment. On a Tuesday morning, Lucy told me that she will be dropping me off at work for the rest of the week. I became agitated and I was surprised by what she just said. I asked, "Why?"

"Because I don't trust you. You're probably going on dates rather than working." She said.

Confused, I looked at her and said, "You can borrow the car if you like. I wouldn't want you to get bored by just staying in the house." Her expressions made me wonder, if this was just a part of her weird sense of humor. But then, her face indicated all seriousness. I went along with it because I didn't want to upset her even more.

On the 28th of July, my birthday, the atmosphere was less tense, and

Lucy was being extra nice. She woke up early and bought breakfast with my debt card. She got me a sausage, egg, and cheese bagel. And she had a plain bagel with yogurt and coffee. She knew that this was one of my favorite sandwiches because I mentioned it a few times in the past. After sitting down at the table, we began to eat.

While we were eating, she asked, "What do you want to do today?"

"To be happy... No problems, no bullshit, and no negativity for the next 24 hours. And if we feel any of these begin to arise, please hold it until the next day." I said. She glanced at me, rolled her eyes, and mumbled under her breath. After a moment, I gave her a "side hug" and left for work.

When I got home, I asked Lucy if she would like to go out for dinner to celebrate my birthday. I had a long day and I still wanted to do something fun. She agreed and we went to a bar called Mezzo's. As I ordered my first drink, I began to look at my phone. It was vibrating and lighting up because I was receiving an abundant amount of birthday texts. My phone did this constantly. I opened all my social media platforms and saw the love everyone was showing me. Lucy's eyes began to swell up like the turkeys from South Park. The wrinkles on her nose began to crease at a fast rate. She snatched my phone from the table and held it in the air.

"I'm going to break this shit!" She shouted!

I said, "Yo! It's all good. I'm receiving birthday messages. I'll show you." I didn't have a password on my phone because I knew she wanted easy access to it. She also told me in the past, if I do not have anything to hide, she should be able to pick it up whenever. I was a good man. Although we were not official, I did not talk to anyone else. She unlocked my phone and started reading my birthday text messages out loud. She began naming who the messages were from and reading them in a wicked witch voice. "Ah, Jessica Flowers 778 said, Happy Birthday Justin! Have an awesome day! Olivia Fit Yoga said, Happy Birthday my friend…" I asked her if my birthday wish was still on the table. The wish that I had requested in the beginning of our day. The "To be happy… No problems, no bullshit, and no negativity for the next 24 hours. And if we feel any of these begin to arise, please hold it until the next day."

She stopped, looked at me and said, "Fuck you!

She threw my phone at me. I paid our tabs and we left. When we got back to the car, Lucy was still furious.

"All I wanted for my birthday was to have a stress-free day. And that didn't happen." I said to her.

Lucy began to shout at me, grabbed my shirt-collar, and said, "Fuck you and your ex-wife. She should never write you anything. Especially, "Happy birthday." Who the heck does she thinks she is? Your friend? I don't even know why you still have her number."

I shook my head because Lucy knew that she is not just my ex-wife but also the mother of my daughter. I had explained this to her when I first met her. When we got back to my place, I hopped in the shower, and let the water run down my face.

Damn…It's only been 3 weeks but it's time for her to go home. I thought. The next day, Lucy acted as if nothing ever happened. She started behaving in a friendly manner and even gave me a hug. I told her that I'm not kicking her out, but feel free to leave whenever. And then I went off to work.

CHAPTER 4

WHO ARE THEY GOING TO BELIEVE?

"How was your day?" Lucy asked. I was surprised by this question. Being confused, I gleamed a quick smile back at her.

"Fine. How was yours?" I replied.

"Great." She said. Lucy stood from the edge of the bed, and whipped out a large white envelope, and hurled it at me.

She held it up to her chest and said, "I did some exploring today and guess what? The courthouse is right down the street. I was able to pick up a few things and this envelope being one of them." I kept looking at it and wondered what was inside.

"Well, what's inside the envelope?" I said.

"Would you get paid more if we were married?" Lucy asked.
"Yes, but why are you asking me this question? I asked. She just smiled at me like the Grinch when he stole Christmas. If you're thinking of what I am thinking, then that would be a hard pass. I do not see myself getting married anytime soon. And plus, marrying for benefits is illegal." I replied. She frowned and I watched as her mood changed drastically. She looked at me like Michael Myers. Lucy stared violently as if she was going to chop my head off.

"I'm going to whoop your ass!" She yelled. Lucy threw the envelope at me and started shouting. I backed up out of the room slowly, looking back and forth at Lucy and my path. "Lucy, what's wrong? Chill out for a minute." I said. She kept walking towards me like T1000 from the Terminator.

"What am I doing here? What is this? What are we?" She shouted. Lucy picked up the envelope off the floor and kept throwing it at me. She repeated this process a few times. When I reached the other side of the room, my back was against the wall and lucy started swinging at me. I guarded myself and managed to escape her tornado of blows. She started rattling about how she dropped everything just to be here. I made it to the door and left immediately. I went outside for a walk. And when I got back, I heard her on speaker phone talking to her brother. "We should just get a place together. I am ready to leave like ASAP." Lucy said. At the time, her brother was going through a nasty divorce and was coaching her on how to drain my pockets. "Look, get everything you can from him, empty his bank account, and ditch him. He is paid! He's in the military!" Lucy's brother said. After hearing that conversation, my mind wasn't focused solely on what Lucy's brother said, but how she mentioned she was ready to leave ASAP. I was feeling excited because I would no longer have to deal with her ever again. I mean, I could have easily kicked her out, but her story was convincing. And sometimes, pitiful. She would say on most days about how much most of her family hated her. Especially her mom. And if she went back, she would probably end up staying on a friend's couch. Her brother was one of the few relatives she had, that would have her back. A few minutes later, I walked in, and Lucy hung up the phone. She looked at me and said, "I will be out of here, but I just need a few more weeks." I stopped and calculated in my head, "I have a work trip coming up...A few more weeks, plus the days of my work trip, converted into Justin minus Lucy equals happiness." Lucy stared at me and was waiting for an answer.

"I am cool with that. I have a work trip coming up anyways." I replied. "Great...STOP! Wait! Did you just say, you have a work trip coming up?" Lucy said.

"I'll be out of town for a week." I said.

"Well, what am I going to do without a car? I don't have any money...How am I supposed to make it?" She said. And started crying. I began to feel so thoughtless and felt sorry for her.

"Well, would you like to come with me?" I said. I was feeling remorse about the whole situation. I felt a relief when she agreed and became calm. A few days later, we drove to Maine without any drama. In

41

fact, the first few days were fine but on the third night, all hell broke loose.

I left work early because I was thinking about keeping Lucy company. In other words, I did not finish all my work and decided to bring it to the hotel. Lucy was standing in the doorway with a bottle of red wine. It looked like she finished most of it. "I poured you a glass. Its right next to the cheese and crackers I was eating on the table." She said.

"Awesome and thank you. I will join you in a bit." I said. I began to set up my work lap-top on the desk near the window. I was eager to have my work completed. It wasn't much and I knew I could knock it out within 30 minutes. She got up from the bed, stared at me like the snake from the jungle book, held her bottle of wine, and said, "Close that shit. Let's drink."

"30 minutes." I told her as I explained intently that I had a few tasks to close out. She walked up to me, nudged me with the bottle of wine, and held it next to my ear.

"Drink!" She commanded. I looked at her briefly and locked my eyes on my screen.

Before a blink of an eye, I started seeing a flash of white strokes in the air and felt a very sharp pain across my right cheek. Lucy slapped me like Will Smith did to Chris Rock during the Oscars. It sounded like an audience applauding a magician that just made a head disappear.

Lucy backed up and said, "When I tell you to drink, you drink!!!"

I sat in the chair for a moment, touched my cheek, and walked towards her slowly. She stared back at me but looked like she was ready to throw down like a UFC fighter before a match. I spread my arms wide and gave her a gentle hug.

"Don't ever put your hands on me or anyone, ever again." I said. I released the hug, sat down, and continued working.

"That's it?" She said, standing and staring at me.

"What do you mean, that's it?" I asked.

"You're not going to hit me?" She asked. I paused, looked at the ground, and then looked at her.

"No, I am not going to hit you." I said in a calm manner.

"My mother said, all black men hit their women." She announced.

"Sorry that your mother thinks that way." I replied.

Lucy began to laugh like "The Predator" from the late 80's movie, starring Arnold Schwarzenegger. She held the bottle of wine at her side. "Are you ok?" I asked.

She said, "The cops...Ha-ha. The cops...Who are they going to believe, a nice blonde, white woman, or a black man?"

CHAPTER 5

DON'T BE PART OF THE PROBLEM, BE THE SOLUTION"
- DR. WAYNE DYER

When we got back to New York from my work trip, things were much drier and duller. The atmosphere felt dark and gloomy. I kept my distance and avoided Lucy as much as possible. I was just patiently waiting for her to pack and leave. My schedule was simple. At 5:00 AM, I woke up and hit the gym till 7:30 AM. I left the gym, got back home to clean up and headed in to work before 9:00 AM. My working hours were from 9:00 AM to 4:00 PM. After work, I'd hit the gym again, from 5:00 PM until 7:00 PM or so. I got home around 7:30 PM, ate dinner, cleaned up, and went to bed around 10:00 PM. This routine was highly effective when it came to avoiding Lucy. I only had to see her in small sections throughout the day. Between us, things were moving along just as planned. "Smooth sailing." I was able to use my own car and drive to and from work each day. As the days went by, I became more anxious and excited for Lucy's departure date. Until one day, Lucy decided to create a ruckus. I think it was her mission to start an argument out of thin air because she was not receiving my attention.

"I can't eat this shit! Why is there so much healthy crap in the fridge? I need a damn car! I need to drive to the grocery store and shit to get some real food. I need some money!!!" Lucy shouted. "You can use the car if you like. The spare key is always sitting on the counter, next to the front door.

And here's $500. I hope this can hold you down for a few weeks." I said.

"I am always bored in this stupid house. I don't have any friends, and I don't know where to go!" Lucy said.

"The local bar and places to eat are only a 5-minute walk down the street. I am sure you can meet some cool people there. You should check it out sometime." I recommended with a smile on my face.

"All of that sounds dumb! I'm not going to walk anywhere. And I most certainly will not hang out with some random strangers at a bar." Lucy said.

"Well played, well played Lucy. You started an argument out of thin air. Mission accomplished." I said to myself. After hearing this, I stopped giving her suggestions. And she continued to complain and say rude things to me on a daily basis.

"The navy is stupid. Why do we even have one anyways? And your uniform is ugly by the way. The colors don't go together." Lucy said this as I walked through the front door. I would just look at her, give a fake nod, and keep moving. I kept my mind on getting in and out of the house as fast as I could. The less time I spent around Lucy, the better.

On most days, Lucy would leave the house a mess and expect me to clean it up. She got me on that one because I could not focus when my living space is messy. She knew that a messy house was one of my pet peeves. Whenever I was in the house, I would notice that she would pile up several dishes. This would occur daily. Whenever I got home from work, the first thing I would do was wash all of Lucy's dishes. Lucy would just watch me and play on her phone. She would occasionally walk near me with trash and drop it on the floor, break crumbs off things she was eating and toss it in front of me. She would say, "You missed a spot."

"When the problem arises, go within. Don't be part of the problem, be the solution." – Dr. Wayne Dyer. When things were getting too tough for me, I would think about this quote. Sometimes it would give me strength and sometimes it would drive me crazy. "How can I go within? What the heck is within when you come home to someone talking trash about you every day? What the heck is within when it comes to someone stacking dishes to the ceiling for you to clean up every day? What the heck is within when it comes to someone dropping crumbs on the floor for you to clean up on purpose?" I thought to myself.

"There isn't any more money on this card. Do you have another one?" Lucy asked as she held up my ATM debt card in the air. I patted my pants pocket to feel for my wallet. Once I felt it, I pulled it out of my rear right pocket, and opened it immediately. I noticed that my ATM card was missing. And looked closely at the one Lucy was holding up.

"How did you get that? And what do you mean there isn't any more money on that card?" I asked. She gave me the card, shook her head, through her hands up in the I don't know position, and walked away.

I stood in my kitchen looking at my debt car in silence. "Maybe someone hacked my card and the bank put a freeze on it." That was my first thought. I unlocked my phone and went to my banking app. I logged in and went straight to my checking's account. I saw a negative balance of -$200.

When I reviewed the transaction history, I noticed that $200 has been withdrawn several times throughout the month. I also noticed that $400 was spent at a money gram location a few times.

"What did you buy with my ATM card?" I asked Lucy.

"Groceries dumbass." Lucy said.

I found that odd because the only groceries that we had were the ones that I bought. "I don't feel comfortable with you using my ATM card." I said.

"A matter of fact, give it here!" Lucy said with her right hand out, and palm facing upward.

"Nah. I don't trust you with it. You cleared out my account. What am I supposed to do until payday next week?" I asked. She ignored my question and said, "Ah. I know why you need it so bad. It's because you have other bitches to spend money on." She snatched it from me and walked backwards as she smiled.

"Lucy, the card isn't good if there isn't any money on it." I mentioned.

After shouting at me for a few minutes, Lucy threw my ATM card. It landed on the floor in front of me. I picked it up, brushed it off, and put it in my wallet. After that day, I made it my duty to open another account. One that Lucy wouldn't know about. And transfer a majority of my money to the new one. It sucks that I even had to do this. What was my life coming to? Also, I would give Lucy a couple hundred dollars each pay day. Not including the money, she would randomly ask me for on a daily and use my old ATM card.

"So, when do you plan on leaving Lucy?" I asked.

"I am going to get a job first and then leave when I have enough money." Lucy said.

"Uhh ok? Well at least you will be making your own money." I said.

She looked at me and smirked. I was happy for her and cheered her on for thinking about getting a job in a sarcastic manner. I also thought about how she would be out of the house more often. "Maybe I won't come home to some bullshit every day after all." I thought to myself.

"Good for you Lucy." I said. She didn't seem as happy as I was but oh well. I learned that she never looks happy so I couldn't tell if she was anyways. I was also hoping that her schedule would keep her so busy that she wouldn't have time to see me. Which means, freedom. Freedom is all I ever wished for since I met Lucy. I felt like mine was taken as soon as she stepped into my life.

I used to beat myself up over the thought of meeting her. I learned that the word, "bored" can get me in trouble. At times, I felt like my patience was being tested by the higher power. I felt like I was being taught a lesson that I can use for the future. "How can I use this? Why was I given such a difficult task that was breaking me down mentally?" I thought to myself.

But don't get me wrong, when Lucy was nice, she was nice. I was allowed to sleep in the bed that I paid for. She would give me hugs and occasionally watch a few shows with me in the living room. I would sometimes hear her laugh and thought to myself, "Maybe she is cool. I need to make adjustments towards what she likes so she can be happy all the time." Later, I found out that she didn't like me at all. And for me to tailor myself to her liking would be a complete waste of time.

For the most part, I was terrified because I felt like Lucy was up to something sneaky. I became very cautious after the remark she made about the cops. "Who are they going to believe, a blonde, white woman. Or a black man." I felt like it was her mission to put me behind bars. I felt like she wanted to ruin my life because I did not want anything to do with her.

One day, her brother sent a text message and after reading it, Lucy started laughing hysterically. Surprised, I looked at her and wondered what was going through her mind.

"So, what's so funny? I asked her.

Lucy said, "My brother sent a text message saying, "Lucy, if you were to have a kid with that black guy you're staying with, how can others tell if the father is black...? He wouldn't be in the picture."

I just gazed at her. After saying that, she began to tell me how racist her family was. She told me her grandmother hated black people with a passion and she would not like me. Lucy said that I would have to also watch out for her grandmother's boyfriend if we were to ever visit them. She said he was a racist old man with no legs. He was a hoarder that would leave piss bottles and trash around the house. "And I know you do not like trash or a messy place. So, in other words, you would be cleaning up since you're so good at it." She said.

Later, Lucy told me her
mother would use the N word frequently.
She said her mother hated all black people.
Lucy's mother wanted her to be with a white
Mormon man. She would call Lucy often
and she would tell me how her mother
wanted her to find a Mormon church
because that is where she may find her
Mormon man. As you may know by now,
Lucy's mom hates that she is in the same
room as me. Lucy started sharing stories
about how her mom didn't care for them
growing up. She shared many stories but the
one that stood out the most was, a story
about carving pumpkins.

"I was carving pumpkins one day and I cut
myself pretty deep. Blood was gushing out
and I called my mom to tell her what had
happened. I told her that I needed a ride to
the hospital, and I cut myself pretty bad."
Lucy said.

"And what did your mom say?" I asked.

"I am baking cookies. And hung up. She let me bleed for a few hours until I decided to give her a call again. And when I did, she was upset because she had more cookies to make." Lucy said.

Lucy also informed me that her brothers were not too fond of African Americans as well. She said, "The only person that might like you is my dad." She told me her dad was an alcoholic and a pervert, but he was a man with a good heart. Lucy said every time she visited him, he was drunk off tequila shots and sometimes he tried to squeeze her butt and breasts.

Confused I said, "What? I can't even imagine." I felt like Lucy was just trying to make me hate her family for no reason. I felt like this was another one of her schemes to make me feel some type of way.

"So, why are you telling me all of this?" I asked.

"I just thought I'd let you know." Lucy said and smiled.

CHAPTER 6

"IF YOU GIVE A CHICKEN RICE, HE'S GOING TO EAT IT." – MOM

Around October, Lucy began to be pretty cool. I was surprised and blown away by her new attitude towards me. We had casual conversations and even hung out more than usual. "What is this sorcery?" I said to myself. On a couple occasions, we ended up in the same bed. This would usually happen after leaving a bar. Although I did not like her much both physically nor mentally, I just went along with it. I remembered thinking about a statement my mother once said, "If you give a chicken rice, he's going to eat it."

There were so many things wrong with this situation. But one thing that made me scratch my head was, Lucy always wanted to spend time with me on a "Tuesday." Not Wednesday, not Thursday, not Friday. It had to be Tuesday. It seemed really odd but as a guy, I was just thinking with a different tool I had. Whenever I got the chance to get down and dirty with her, I took the opportunity. Stupidly, I didn't think about the consequences I may face in the future. Her "Down and dirty" was not anything special but it was something. I should say, "It was something to do when I got bored." If I could describe it, I would say, "A dead smelly fish."

Many times, I would just handle business in the restroom. Hey they say, "If you don't use it, you lose it." Or do they say, "You must be bored?" Lucy would bang on the door and say, "You don't have to do that. I'm here. And plus, it is Tuesday..." I finished up, washed my hands, and went to bed. The next day when I came home from work, I heard Lucy talking to a male on speakerphone. She was telling him how much she did not like me and how she cannot wait to get back home to hang out with him. I wasn't shocked at all. In fact, I was thrilled. I opened the door and Lucy took her phone off speaker, told the male that she would call him back, and hung up immediately. I asked Lucy who was she was talking to, and she said, "Does it matter?" And I said, "Nah. Never mind because it doesn't matter." She smiled at me and asked, "What? Are you jealous? I kind of like that. It shows that you care." I looked at her with a smirk on my face. I shook my head and went into the living room. Later that night, I received a text message from one of my female coworkers stating a change in our schedule.

Lucy snatched my phone and asked,
"Who the heck is this? Who is texting you?"
She licked her lips as she scrolled through
my text messages. Before she gave me my
phone back, she turned on my location and
sent the pin to her phone. This allowed her
to track me all the time.

"Lucy, what's this? What did you do to my
phone?" I asked.

"I turned your location on because I don't
trust you with these bitches." Lucy shouted.

"They are my co-workers. But whatever.
You already track my every move on
Snapchat anyways." I said.

Did it make a difference for her to have
another app that can track me? Not at all. I
felt like a prisoner anyways. Whenever I
received a text message from my female

coworkers or the ex-wife, Lucy would snatch my phone and reply to them. I wouldn't realize until I would re-read my messages and notice that things were sent on her behalf. Sometimes my co-workers would stare at me funny and later ask, "Why would you say something like that?" Most of the time I was confused until I would check my phone. "Hey my bad. I was hacked by Lucy again." I said to my co-workers. I told them a little bit about what was going on at home. I did this just in case I did not show up for work one day, I would hope they would check on me. This whole situation started getting pretty bad. So bad to the point that Lucy changed all my passwords to my social media platforms and attempted to log in whenever she pleased. If I "liked" a picture of a fitness model while I was at work, I would be coming home to a screenshot of what I "liked" and greeted with an argument that always started out like the following:

"Who is this bitch?" She would hold her phone up to my face and grab my clothing as if she was going to tear it off me. This definitely broke me down mentally because I was not prepared for a battle like this. This was the first time I went into a war with my hands tied down. I felt like a hobbit. I never fought back and just hid most of the time. I did this because I did not know what else to do. I did this because I was being extra cautious. I did not want to give her the upper hand for any situation. I know I brought this up quite a few times but the "Who are they going to believe?" situation paralyzed my tactics. My thought process was, she cannot manipulate my actions if I don't give her any. Lucy would run my social media for the most part. She said, if I'm going to post pictures, she better be in most of them. We barely took pictures and when we did, they weren't very pleasant. On many occasions, she would log into my

Instagram account and create posts of us together. She would create her own custom captions to make it seem like we were in love. The captions would resemble as the following:

Caption 1: "I am so happy to be with Lucy."
Caption 2: "She is the best thing that has ever happened to me."
Caption 3: "Just here spending time with the love of my life."

I felt so weird and sick to my stomach every time she created a post. My friends would reply to her captions and write half ass comments like, "Happy for you. Good deal. Nice bro. Whipped." The difficult part was a lot of different friends would write each time. And it was hard to keep up with them. I had to use my work phone or email them secretly to let them know that my social media was compromised by Lucy. I also told them not to write me on any platform until I get things sorted out. Most of the people that I talked to thought I was joking. I felt like everything that I had personally, was being overrun by Lucy. She was acting like an intruder, forcing herself into my life and specifically, my private affairs. I no longer knew what privacy meant within my life. I felt like a slave, under the supervision of a cruel master who had no mercy. I felt like an abused dog locked up in a crate, craving freedom, and peace. It was hard for me to focus at work because I wasn't getting enough sleep at home. I was constantly on my toes. Sometimes, I would slumber at work, and I would crave to lay in a bed or a flat surface for just 5 minutes. This situation affected my overall wellbeing. My work performance went downhill, and I struggled to get things done. And that has never been part of me. I am a go getter. I get things done. And if I didn't, I would find a way to. Except in this situation, the "Go getter" mindset was thrown out the window. I talked to one of my coworkers about my situation and they recommended that I seek help. I called military one source and they assigned me a psychologist by the name of Dr. Light. I desired to have my own privacy again and to be free. I was looking forward to meeting Dr. Light. "Maybe this could be it. Maybe this could be the cure to happiness. Maybe this could help me find the "Within" that Dr. Wayne Dyer was talking about." I thought to myself.

CHAPTER 7

DR. LIGHT

Dr. Light was a psychologist that specialized in couple's therapy. From what I heard; he was pretty good at what he does. Even though Lucy and I were not a couple, I asked her if she would like to join me for therapy.

"That is the dumbest shit ever." Lucy said.

I wasn't shocked to hear this at all.
"Well, you're welcome to join me if you change your mind. I am leaving in about 30 minutes." I said. When it was time to leave. Lucy followed me to the car and got in.

"I'm going." Lucy said. I looked at her for a moment as I put my seatbelt on.

"Cool." I said as I started the engine and backed out of my parking spot.

We headed to Dr. Lights office. When we got there, I told the receptionist we had an appointment with Dr. Light. She checked us in and said, "He will be with you shortly." We sat down for a few minutes and saw a man with a white beard, white hair, glasses, and a lab coat. "Justin? Hi, I am Dr. Light. Nice to meet you guys." He said. We shook his hand and then followed him to his back office. To me, he seemed like a nice guy who wore a warm smile on his face. His office was small but tidy. And I noticed that he had U.S. Navy insignias posted on a few of his walls. Just by seeing that, I felt a great bond. "This is going to be a fun session." I said to myself.

When we began our session, I began to tell him a little bit about what was going on. I talked about my freedom, how Lucy treats me, and how all of this was interfering with my work life. Hearing this, Lucy started crying like a sad frog from a Disney movie. I became silent for a moment and looked at

71

her. Dr. Light looked at me and said, "Can you please excuse us for a bit?" I stood up, fixed my coat, and said, "Sure. Not a problem."

I sat outside for about 20 minutes and then Lucy opened the door. She stepped out and walked towards me as she wiped her red eyes saying, "You're fucked. Oh and Dr. Light wants to see you." She smirked and gave me a little smile as she watched me walk into Dr. Light's office.

I looked at Dr. Light and he had a weird smile on his face. It looked like he smelled his own fart and liked it. I was confused as I sensed the vibes in the room have changed from the previous feeling.

"So, tell me more about what's going on?" Dr. Light said.

I was going to tell him about Lucy putting her hands on me, but I figured I'd wait until next time.

"Well, I feel like I am a slave. Lucy is controlling, she makes me send her my location, she replies to my co-workers when they text me, she logs into my social media and pretends to be me. I can go on." I said. I looked at Dr. Light and I can tell he wasn't interested in anything else that I had to say. He kept looking at his clock. So, I started talking about the military.

"So, did you serve in the Navy as well?" I asked.

"Yes. I did 4 years and decided it wasn't for me. I used to work on radio's." Dr. Light said as he yawned for the 10th time. Dr. Light paused and said, "Well, it looks like our time is up. Let's continue this next week."

I shook his hand and left. I saw Lucy in the waiting room and went up to her. "Are you ready?" I asked. Lucy did not say a word and walked out. When we made it to my car, I unlocked it, opened Lucy's door, and closed it after she got in. I walked around to the driver's side, took a deep breath, let it out, and went into my car. As soon as my door shut, I looked over at Lucy. And she began laughing like a hyena. I was confused. I asked her in a nervous manner if she was ok. I was worried this therapy session did damage rather than repair our situation. I stared at Lucy and was expecting a response. She continued to laugh and look out the window. I put the car in drive and drove towards my apartment.

"Dr. Light called you dandy! Ha-ha. Oh, and he thinks you're an asshole." She said.

Of course, I did not believe her.

"Why were you crying during the session?" I asked.

Lucy said, "You just don't get it do you? What an idiot." She said.

We got to the house, and I sat in the living room alone. I thought to myself, why is she doing this to me? What does she want from me? I never knew people like her existed within this world. She was driving me crazy, and I just wanted her to leave. But most of all, I wanted my freedom back.

After cooling off, I asked Lucy, "What do you want from me?"

She immediately yelled, "I just want what you and Mary have!"

For a brief moment, there was nothing but silence. Mary is my ex-wife. We met in the seventh grade, talked a little bit throughout our high school years and ended up together at the end of high school. We have a daughter, and we were married for six years. Our life was pretty good. But I divorced her after my second deployment. Although My ex-wife cheated on me multiple times with girls and guys, drained my bank accounts, emptied my apartment, had sex in the same bed my daughter was sleeping in, manipulated me the whole time, tried to have sexual intercourse with my sister's fiancé, and a ton of other things, I

75

forgave her. We left on good terms and managed to have a great co-parenting relationship for a while. I pondered why Lucy would want what my ex-wife and I had? She doesn't even know what we have.

I looked at Lucy and said, "What Mary and I had, you and I will never have. And I am sure you wouldn't want it anyways."

Lucy slapped me across the face, pulled my shirt and continue to send slaps left and right while cursing me out. I ducked and managed to escape with my car keys. When I got to my car, I looked in the mirror and saw minor scratches on my face, neck, and arms.

I shrugged it off with a smile and said to myself…Damn, what have I gotten myself into…

CHAPTER 8

NICE GIFTS

It was a Saturday morning, and I woke up to hearing Lucy saying, "I have to go to work from 9:00 AM until 11:00 AM." She demanded to use my car.

"Just to let you know, I am on standby this weekend. And most likely, I have to be in by noon." I said. She knows, I usually get called into work, once a month on the weekends.

She stared at me for a few seconds and said, "I'm taking the freakin' car! I will only be gone for a few hours." I just looked at her as she walked towards the front door. Lucy looked back at me like a Japanese Hannya mask character, grabbed the keys and slammed the door.

"What an idiot! If he bought me a car, I wouldn't be in this situation." She said to herself as she left the apartment.

I heard the car start up, and Lucy pealed out of the parking space like a Sega Rally Championship NASCAR driver. I looked up at the sealing as if I was going to find a magical answer to my thought of, "Why the heck is this woman so angry?" I laughed and then decided to go for a morning run. I went into my room, opened my dresser, and pulled out my favorite black tank top, some black shorts, and my black Nike Zooms. As I changed, I looked in the mirror and said to myself, "Since I am wearing black, you know what that means…I am going to murder this workout." I was just getting my mind prepared for what I will accomplish. I stepped outside, conducted some static stretching, and began to walk down the street for two minutes. Once I felt like I was ready to run, I started the timer on my watch and began picking up speed. Whenever I would run, I'd get a burst of joy that I cannot explain. At times, I would forget about every worry in the world. Whenever I felt down, I would go for a run. And being with Lucy, I was running a lot. I always looked forward to running because I felt like my life wouldn't be the same without it. When I was approaching my tenth-mile, sweat was pouring down my face, neck, and back. I slowed down because my music was interrupted by a call from work.

"Hey my man! We need you to stop by the office for a bit. It shouldn't take all day." My co-workers said.

"I will be there around 12:30 PM." I said. Beep…Beep…Beep…My watch notified me that I just hit the ten-mile mark. I turned around and decided to take a short cut back home because I needed time to get ready. I cut through the city, hopped a few fences, and made it back home by 11:00 AM. Before I got into the shower, I texted Lucy the following:

"I got the call. I have to be at work at 12:30 PM. Good thing you're off at 12 and right down the street. See you shortly."

Lucy read my message immediately but did not reply. I put my phone down, took a shower, and got ready. I ate breakfast, cleaned up the house, and went into the living room to sit down. I checked my phone to see if Lucy wrote back but she didn't. It was 11:30 AM and I was getting nervous. I texted Lucy again saying, "Just let me know what your plan is and if you're going to be here by 12 or so." She read my message again but did not reply. I was most certainly not going to depend on her.

I looked at my Nike Zooms and smiled. "My worksite is 10 miles away. If I leave now, I can be there by 12:30 PM." I said to myself. I changed clothes, stuffed my uniform in a backpack, and slipped my Nike's on. I picked up my backpack, fastened it, turned my headphones on, and grabbed a bottle of water. As soon as I left my apartment, I began jogging at a faster pace than usual. The roads were narrow, but I managed to maneuver around oncoming traffic. One hour later, I arrived at my worksite and was greeted by one of my co-workers. "Look at you Ironman! Running to work because you are hardcore! When I grow up, I want to be like you." My co-worker said sarcastically.

"Lucy has my car…" I said. My co-worker looked at me for a moment, shook his head, and kept walking into the building. When I got to my desk, my other co-workers said we have a teleconference. And it should only last 15 minutes.

"You mean to say, you called me to come in when I could have just dialed in?" I said to my co-workers as I stared at them.

"Uhh…I didn't look at it that way but yes. Yes, that is correct." I shook my head and didn't bother to change clothes. After the teleconference, one of my co-workers dropped me off at home. I loved running but not that much. I would have put in 30 miles if I ran back. I thanked my co-worker for his kind gesture and waved as he took off. Lucy pulled in and parked right in front of me. She got out of the car and rushed to the backseat to grab a few bags of stuff.

"Hi Lucy. Do you need help?" I asked. She gathered up all the bags and sped past me. Her hands were full, so I rushed to the front door to open it for her. She walked in without saying a thing. I looked at her as I closed the door and said, "You're welcome."

"What are you looking at?" Lucy said.

"You know, I had to be at work today and I almost didn't make it. If I didn't run, I wouldn't have been there." I said.

"Well who was that who dropped you off?" Lucy said.

"That was Petty Officer First Class Smith." I said.

"Well good for you. You got a

workout in." Lucy said in a sarcastic manner as she put her bags down. I was a little irritated by her actions, but I kept my composure. I changed the subject for a moment and said, "Nice gifts." As I pointed at her bags.

"They are for my family." Lucy said.

"Good stuff. And by the way, you're the one who needs to put your location on. If I knew where you were, I could have picked up my car." I said in a jokingly manner. She sent her location to me and said, "There, you have it now. Happy?" I stopped and looked at her with confusion on my face.

"You didn't have to do that. I was just playing around." I said. She walked away and I hopped in the shower. All I could think about was eating a big, juicy burger, pizza, in fact, anything. I didn't notice but all I ate was a light breakfast. And since I did so much running, my body was craving a large meal. When I was done, I dried off, and opened the restroom door. I noticed that Lucy was gone once again. I didn't mind her being gone but when I looked in the fridge, I didn't have much. My stomach growled and my feet were too sore to run another mile. "What time will you be back? I'm starving and would like to get a bite to eat. Let me know if you're down." I texted Lucy. A few hours went by, and she still did not reply. I sat and thought, "What the heck is she up to?" And then I remembered she sent me her location. I grabbed my phone and tapped on her location. I notice she was parked at a nearby restaurant. I called Lucy and she did not pick up. I sent a text saying, "Yo, I am hungry. Can you at least bring me back something to eat?" She just ignored me. I was annoyed and most of all "Hangray." I looked over at   her gifts and came up with the dumbest idea. Since she was getting under my skin, the least I could do is play her game with her. I tore off pieces of the wrapping paper and stacked them on top of each other in a messy form. I staged it as if I destroyed and unwrapped her packages. Nothing was broken. I just made it appear to be. I laughed and said, "Yeah, have fun re-wrapping." I knew wrapping presents was not her favorite thing to do but she managed to make it happen. I figured it took her a long ass time since they were wrapped so neatly. I said, "Waste my time, I will waste yours." It felt pretty good dumbing down to her level during that moment. After, I decided to put my running shoes on yet again and headed her way. When I got there, I saw Lucy sitting at a table by herself with two drinks and two meals. I walked into the restaurant, and she looked up at me quickly.

"Hey…" I said.

"You're using your location app I see." Lucy said.

"Yeah. Since you enjoy ignoring my text messages. I don't have time for this nonsense. Especially when it comes to food." I said. She smiled and handed me my keys. We got into the car, and I drove back to the apartment. My goal was to drop her off, make a quick restroom stop, and grab the burger that I was daydreaming about. When we got to the house, I told her that I did something that she is not going to like. She looked at me like a demon and said, "What?" I said to myself, "I can play your game as well." I opened the door and waited for her reaction. But it was something complete opposite of what I was expecting.

She stopped in the doorway and said, "What the hell did you do?" She took out her phone, walked over to the gifts, and started taking pictures. Lucy paused and then began recording and started crying dramatically.

She yelled, "Oh my god! How could you do this?" She would pause, fix her camera, fix her hair, and then begin to "fake cry" even louder as she created her footage.

I walked over to her and said, "Look, nothing is broken. I just tore up the wrapping paper. It's all staged. Here, I will help you rewrap them." Lucy pushed me away. She began to crush the gifts and throw them at me. I caught a few, put them on the ground, and tried to dodge her but she continued to create a storm. Lucy stomped on each package, shouted like a werewolf, and kept slamming the smaller gifts like a rockstar breaking his guitar. I stopped and watched from a distance. Lucy picked up a stuffed animal that was in one of the boxes, looked over at my scissors sitting on the table, and attempted to cut the head off. Once she found a stopping point, she began recording and fake crying again. "How could you? How could you do this?" She said. That is when I knew, she was trying to stage all of this non-sense. I learned that my plan to "play her game," backfired ten times harder.

"Lucy, I am sorry for touching your gifts. I shouldn't have unwrapped them. And because of that, I'll rewrap them for you next time." I said. I reached into my wallet and handed her $300. "Here, this should take care of this mess. My apologies once again." I said. She looked at me with her red eyes and began to smile.

"And you are going to buy them all new gifts right?" She asked.

"I just gave you $300. But I guess?" I said.

"Ok. Leave me the fuck alone now." Lucy shouted.

I looked around the room and notice that she bought her brother a cheap record player, her mother a stuffed animal, her dad a few candles and her youngest brother a beanie. All of this was under $100. I knew it because she used my debit card to pull out money and purchase these items. For the next few days, I kept my distance to the maximum. I also felt like I had to sleep with one eye open because there was no telling what she would do next. I left the apartment and finally got my burger that I was yearning for. I shook my head, took a sip of my beer, and thought about the whole situation. "Did I handle that wisely? Did I mess up? When Lucy talks about this situation, who are they going to believe?"

CHAPTER 9

GTA

One evening after work, I changed into my gym clothes as fast as I could because I had to take a piss. I was also trying to avoid Lucy at all costs. This happened to be my evening routine on most days. Lucy was in the living room watching TV. But before I could leave, she stopped me in the kitchen.

"I need to use the car. I need to go to the mall to grab a few things." Lucy stated.

"Ok? Well, I am going to the gym right now. How about I take you when I get back? I'm only doing cardio tonight and should be done within an hour or so. And plus, I need to hit the mall as well." I said.

"COULD YOU NOT?" Lucy shouted.

"Lucy, I will take you after." I said kindly as I proceeded to go into the restroom before leaving. As I emptied the tank, I thought to myself, "I seriously do not feel like going anywhere with Lucy but a quick run to the mall, after the gym should be a breeze. By being in the same room with her over 5 minutes, I felt like I had to mentally prepare myself. I took a deep breath, flushed the toilet, put the seat down, and washed my hands. I stared into the mirror before leaving and said silently, "It's gym time. Let's go!" When I opened the door, it was extremely quiet. The TV was off, and I noticed that my car keys were missing. I heard my car start and I rushed outside. I saw Lucy speeding away as if she was a get-away driver, robbing a bank.

"Damn…" I said as I stared until I couldn't see my car anymore.

"Lucy, I told you I was going to the gym, and I would take you to the mall after. You didn't have to steal my car." I texted her. She read my text message and did not reply back. I waited for a moment and said to myself, "Whatever…I am still going to get my cardio in." I jogged around the neighborhood for a few hours, made it back home, took a shower, ate dinner, and Lucy was still not back. I remember she sent me her pin location a while back and I decided to check it. When I looked on my phone, I noticed that she disabled it. So, I immediately disabled my location. A few seconds later, Lucy called. I picked up and she hung up immediately.

"Since you turned your location off, now I know you're going to hang out with your side chicks. Go ahead!" Lucy texted me.

"Where are you? I need my car." I replied. Since I felt like there was going to be a shit show when she got home, I decided to change, get ready, and walk down to the local bar. I hung out until 1:00 AM because I figured she would be sleeping by the time I got back. I was overwhelmed with hiding, being afraid to spend time at home, not having a safe space, always on the alert, and most of all, anticipating the days until she left. The worst part was, she never gave me an official date of when she will be going home. When I approached my apartment, I noticed that my car was still missing. I opened my front door and noticed that it was unlocked. I saw a trail of trash on the floor, and I immediately searched the place because I thought someone had broken in. When I looked in one of the closets, I noticed that all of Lucy's belongings were missing. I kind of smiled and felt an abundant amount of weight lifted from my shoulders. But then, I instantly felt the weight drop on top of my head, awakening me from this beautiful feeling. "Dude! She still has your car!" I said to myself. I grabbed my phone and called her a few times. I texted her saying, "Lucy, you need to return my car ASAP. I have to go to work in a few hours." I sat down on the couch, stayed up until 5:00 AM, and ended up falling asleep for a few hours. Beep...Beep...Beep...It was 7:45 AM and I woke up to a few text messages from Lucy.

"I am on my way home. I am at the airport. Your car is parked on the third floor in the daily parking garage. It's in spot C3. The keys are under the rear left tire. You better come and pick it up now because it's racking up money as we speak. Oh, and side note, the sunrise looks beautiful in the morning. You should try to catch a morning flight sometime." I tried to call her, but it went straight to voicemail. I figured she was already on the flight, or she just put her phone on airplane mode so I couldn't contact her. I was not in a good mood due to the lack of sleep and the situation. All I could think about was, "I need my car. I have to be at work in a few hours. The airport was a two-hour drive away and the only people that I knew who might be willing to take me was my co-workers. I looked over at my Nike's and said, "Shall we dance?" I put them on, grabbed my headphones, and headed out the door. I made it to work around 9:00 AM. One of my co-workers was pulling up to the front gate and saw me standing in front of it. "Good morning!" One of my co-workers by the name of Chief Petty Officer Tatum greeted me.

"Hey, morning!" I replied.

"Where is your car?" She asked.

"It's funny that you ask...Lucy took my car to the airport." I said. Tatum shook her head and said, "Well, let's go!" We checked in with the rest of our staff, told them the situation, and took the government vehicle to retrieve my car.

My coworker and I ended up missing work for the rest of the day. When we finally got to the airport, we found my car. I called our Commander to let her know that we are heading back. I put her on speaker phone and held it up so Tatum and I can both hear. Our commander said, "Just go home. You guys have a lot of tasks to make up tomorrow. And I am not very happy that both of you left for the day."

"You can thank Lucy for stealing

your car." Tatum said.

"Yeah…I am just glad she is gone." I said. I got into my car, thanked Tatum for driving me to the airport and said, "See you tomorrow." Tatum gave me a nod and we went our separate ways. On my way back home, I had the biggest smile on my face. I was finally free of Lucy. I felt like I just got back from Iraq. I felt like I just survived hell. I felt like I was able to finally breathe again. I thought about all the things I will be doing as soon as I got back. Relax, meditate, enjoy some quiet time. Geeze, it felt like I haven't done any of those things in years. But in reality, it was only a few months.

When I got home, I cleaned up, washed my sheets, and took a little nap. The peace that I felt around me was blissful. I no longer had to look over my shoulder, I no longer had to worry about someone nagging as soon as I walked through the door, and I no longer felt uncomfortable in my own apartment. This was the feeling that I craved for so long.

Over the course of the next few days, I didn't hear from Lucy until one day, out of the blue…Beep…Beep…Beep…

"Yo." I answered my phone.

"Hey, I might be pregnant." Lucy said.

I laughed, and said, "Awesome. Who is the father?"

"You!" She said.

"Impossible…I barely touched you." I paused. And thought about the few drunken nights we spent together. I thought about how she always invited me into bed on a

"Tuesday." Right then, I realized that she might have trapped me. I didn't stress nor did I argue. Lucy said, "It is yours Justin."

"Let's get a paternity test and let that determine this. And if he or she is mine, you know I will be there." I said.

"I am not asking you to be here. I am just letting you know."
"Like I said, if he or she is mine, I'll be there." I Repeated. To ease the tension, I made a side comment. "So, if it's a girl, we should name her Cali." I chuckled.

"You do not get a say in his or her name. You do not get a say in anything." Lucy said.

"Wait what? So, if the child is mine, it's not going to have my last name?" I asked.

"LIKE I FUCKIN' SAID, YOU DO NOT GET A SAY IN ANYTHING." Lucy shouted and hung up.

"What a douche..." I said as I stared at my phone. As time went by, I would call her often to check on her. Even though I wasn't sure if the child was mine or not, I felt a bond with Lucy and wanted to do something. All I could think about was the child and how fun life would be. All the bad things and crazy times Lucy put me through, flew over my head. I no longer cared about her past actions. My main focus was finding out the truth. Was she really pregnant? Is it really mine? That paternity test couldn't come soon enough. This whole time, I wanted her gone but a piece of me wanted her back. I wanted to work on "Us." Her actions of what she wanted in her mind was turning into a reality. A few weeks later, I cracked open a bottle of wine, drank a glass, and then decided to give her a call. Still awaiting the paternity test results, I asked her an odd question.

"Hello." Lucy answered.

"Hi. So, would you ever want to come back?" I asked.

"If I were to come back, you would have to do a few things for me." She said.

"And what's that?" I replied.

"Apologize to my brother, apologize to my mother, and apologize to me. You can apologize to my family through text but to me, you must do it in person." She said.

"What am I apologizing for? Was it because I ruin the wrapping paper on the gifts?" I asked confusedly.

"No! It's because you didn't treat me right." Lucy said.

"How was I supposed to treat you? Like a Queen?" I said sarcastically. She laughed and said, "Better…"

" I did everything for you. I let you walk on top of me. You had access to my bank account, my car, I gave you money whenever you asked, you ran my social media, you put a tracking device on my phone, you treated me like scum and slapped me around often. What about you? How were you supposed to treat me?"

"Like that because you deserved it." Lucy said. I shook my head and said, "Wow…That's ruthless."

"So, do you want me to come back

101

or not?" Lucy asked. Again, all that nonsense went over my head. The only thing I was thinking about was the baby.

"Yeah. I want you to come back so we can figure things out. Do you want me to call your family right now?" I asked.

"No! No! Just text them. But send it to me first." Lucy said. I wrote a short message saying that I missed Lucy, I hope that she would come back, and if there is anything that they recommend I do in order for that to happen. Still on speaker phone with Lucy, I read my message to her before sending it off, and she said it wasn't good enough. She sent me her version, a cringing version of the message that she wanted me to send to her brother and mother. I do not remember it fully, but I do remember that it made me feel uncomfortable.

"I am sorry for not treating her like a Queen. I am sorry for letting you down. I am sorry for..." Her message read. I remember sitting down and thinking about sending this. I was about to say, "Hell no will I send this awful message to your family." But then again, all I had on my mind was the baby. I was willing to do whatever it took to be part of its life. I also thought, "Would they truly believe that I wrote this? Or would they suspect it was Lucy's idea? Who are they going to believe?"

"Ok, I will send it. Please text me their numbers." I said. Once I got them, I sent the cringing message without hesitation. Lucy's brother and mother read the message immediately and did not respond.

"Done. Are we good now?" I asked.

"Now, you have to apologize to me in person." She said.

CHAPTER 10

WHY DIDN'T YOU CRY?

Before going to California for Christmas break, I previously scheduled a therapy session with Dr. Light.

"Where's Lucy?" Dr. Light asked in a concerned manner.

"She went home. As in, she hopped on a plane and flew to California." I replied.

Dr. Light fixed his glasses, looked at the ground, cleared his throat, and just smiled at me for a moment. "So, tell me what's going on?" He said.

"Well, first of all, Lucy is abusive, she is controlling, she tracks my location, and says racial slurs on a daily basis. We recently had a small argument, she stole my car, dropped it off at the airport, caught a flight, told me that she was pregnant with my child a few weeks after she landed, and then I asked her to come back, and she said only if I do three things for her. And those three things were, apologize to her mother, brother and to her. She created a prewritten text, sent it to me, and said I must send it to her mother and brother individually. Even though it was cringing and would make me look like a fool, I sent it anyway. I told her I would do almost anything to work on "us." Now, that I may possibly have a child with her, all I wanted to do is focus on raising him or her. I currently do not know if he or she is truly mine or not. I have requested a paternity test and still awaiting the results." I said as I watched Dr. Light scribble on his notepad. He looked at me, looked at his clock and gave me a confused smile.

"So, what should I do?" I asked.

"Everything that you are telling me, is what Lucy said you were doing to her. And after hearing your version. It's all starting to make sense. What do you want to happen? Do you plan on being in a relationship with her?" Dr. Light asked. I was beginning to see why Dr. Light looked at me funny in the past. Lucy flipped the script by playing the role of the victim.

"Honestly, all I can think about is the baby. But in reality, I do not ever see myself being in a relationship with her." I said.

Dr. Light looked at his clock, yawned, and scribbled a few more times on his notepad.

When I looked at his notepad, from what I saw, he was writing about things that didn't have to do with what we were talking about. Dr. Light looked up quickly, stretched and yawned once again. I felt like he did not care about our session. So, I changed the subject and started talking about the U.S. Navy.

"So, did you serve as well?" I said as I pointed at one of his military pictures hanging on the wall.

"Oh yes. It was many years ago. I only did four years, got out, and used the G.I. Bill to go to school. And now here I am. Your psychologist." Dr. Light said as he smiled. Talking about the Navy became the highlight of our conversation, and we ended our session by sharing stories about boot camp.

"So, see you next week?" Dr. Light asked.

"Can we schedule for three weeks out? I am heading to California for Christmas break." I asked.

"Oh, that's right. Yes. We can do that. I will send you a confirmation shortly. Have a great time...And one more thing. Can you call Military One Source and ask them to send the payment directly to my personal email address?" Dr. Light mentioned. I looked at him and thought to myself, "Hey, everyone needs to get paid but was that worth the money? Man, I am so glad I am not paying for this out of pocket because I didn't gain anything from our sessions. Except, one thing. And that was to finally tell someone about what I have been holding in for so long.

"Of course I will call Military One Source as soon as I get home. See you soon

Dr. Light." I said. I felt a little hurt knowing that he was my psychologist and spent most of the time looking at the clock, yawning, and couldn't wait to say, "Well, it looks like our time is up." I noticed that his smile was genuine and real after those words left his mouth. I also understood that I was not the only patient he had but just wished he could have at least, acted like he cared. During that time, I felt like I was in this game alone. The only person that knew about this situation was Dr. Light and Lucy. I was about to cancel the rest of our sessions as I kept thinking about how they were going but a piece of me wanted to give Dr. Light a few more shots. And plus, it was nice to have a small get-away and a reason to leave work early, share funny stories, and let out dark secrets that are, "supposedly" confidential on a weekly basis. I ended up calling Military One Source and fulfilled Dr. Lights request.

"When I got to California, I met up with Lucy. The first thing she said was, "I have a doctor's appointment for the baby." "When? And can I go? Do you need a ride?" I asked.

"Bitch, I don't want you to be there. I was just letting you know that I have stuff to do today." Lucy said. I let the "Bitch" comment slide over my head and acted like I didn't hear it. I knew her goal was to see me lose my cool and act like a fool. I also learned that I could not let her actions control mine.

"Well, if he or she is mine, I should be allowed to go." I said.

"The baby is yours you idiot!" Lucy said. She thought for a moment and said, "I do need a ride. You can take me. We need to be in San Diego in one hour or so."

We walked over to my car, got in, and drove to the appointment. When we arrived, I followed Lucy to check in at the front desk.

"And where the fuck are you going?" Lucy said with her red eyes with dark black circles surrounding them. She looked like one of the zombies from the Walking Dead because she barely slept, didn't have a heart, and was full of anger. I wasn't afraid of her, but zombies made me jump. And after looking into her eyes and hearing her speak, all I could think about was getting away from a "Zombie walker."

"Why do you speak to me this way?" I asked. Lucy looked me up and down and continued walking to the front desk. I stopped following her, looked at the waiting area, walked towards it, and decided to sit near the TV. After Lucy checked in, she looked for me, walked over, and sat one empty seat away from me. I unlocked my phone and started randomly deleting useless apps that I didn't use.

"I see you texting all your other bitches." Lucy said.

"What?" I said with confusion. Lucy glared at me and then a few moments later, a nurse came into the waiting room. She had brown hair, light blue scrubs, a well-built physique, and wore black crocks.

"Lucy Dickson?" The nurse called out.

"Here." Lucy said. We got up at the same time and began walking towards the nurse.

"Hey! You can sit your ass back down. You are not coming in the room with me." Lucy said. The nurse looked at her, then looked at me with uncertainty.

"You both can come in." The nurse said with a smile on her face as we followed her through the door. Once we got to the room, the nurse took Lucy's vitals and gave her a gown to change into.

"Please put this on and I will be right back. I am going to see if the doctor is ready for you." The nurse said and shut the door. I felt like I was sitting in a small pool with an alligator that was ready to snap and then...

"GET THE FUCK OUT OF THIS ROOM! You are not about to see me naked!" Lucy yelled. I looked at her confusedly as she hovered over me. Lucy was trying her best to taunt me for some reason. So, I decided to crack a joke.

"Come to think about it, I never saw you naked. I know you're Mormon, and they usually smash through a hole in a sheet. Is that what we did?" I said jokingly as I stood up. Lucy opened the door and pushed me out, and then closed it tight. I looked up and saw a few nurses staring at me.

"Sir, you're supposed to be in the room." The nurse said.

"Lucy kicked me out." I said. All the nurses looked confused, and I proceeded to walk towards the waiting room. When I got there, I sat down and watched TV for 20 minutes.

"Come on! Let's go." Lucy said and she tapped on my left arm. I got up and looked at her. She began speed walking to my car.

"Lucy! Wait up. Is everything ok?" I asked.

"Yeah. I'm all done and just ready to go. Take me to my brothers. Give me your phone so I can put his address in your navigation." Lucy stated. When I dropped her off, she got out of my car and said, "I have another appointment tomorrow. Pick me up at the same time. And get here a little early." I looked at her and said to myself, "Who the heck does she think she is? My Commander?" Never in my life have I ever met someone so rude and demanding. Not even my leaders within the military treated me the way Lucy did. I always thought, deep down there might be a nice woman underneath her, "Captain Demon" attitude. And then I stopped my train of thought and said to myself, "Nahhhh! Even when she appeared to be nice, I was just blind to see like Coolio."

"Sir yes sir! I will be picking you up

tomorrow, 15 minutes prior." I said in a jokingly manner and gave her a salute. Lucy looked at me, shook her head and walked away. I drove to Oceanside to visit my mother. When I got there, she gave me a big hug.

"Justin! It's so nice to see you!" My mother said. She looked at me and her whole vibe changed. I felt like all the lights turned off and it was just my mother and I in a dark room.

"Son, what happened? Are you ok?" She asked.

"It's Lucy...Ever since she stepped into my life, I felt it all turn upside down. She has been abusing me, controlling my social media, tracking me, taking over my apartment, my car, my debit card, and the worst part is...She might be pregnant." I announced.

"I knew there was something wrong when I heard your voice every time you called." My mother replied. She gave me a hug and said, "Don't worry. Everything is going to work out. Storms do not last forever. And if you need anything, call me. I will always be here for you." I was crying inside because I felt alone until I heard these words. I didn't know what I was doing at times. I questioned life and occasionally said to myself, "Why did Lucy choose me? Why?"

"Thank you mom. You're the best." I said as I gave her a hug. She smiled, got up, and began cooking my favorite dish. "Spaghetti." My mother always knew how to take my mind off any situation. And that was "food." We ate and after a few hours, I ended up passing out on the couch until the next morning. I woke up around 8:00 AM, hit the beach for a long jog, took a shower, and ate breakfast. After, I looked at the time and made my way to pick up Lucy. I texted her, "On my way." She read it and didn't reply. When I got there, she was waiting outside. I parked, turned the car off, got out of the car, smiled, and opened her door.

"Your chariot awaits you." I said with a Roman Soldier accent.

"Really? Are you going to keep this up?" Lucy said with her eyes bulging out like a squid.

"You can open your own door next time." I said in a teasing manner. I was beginning to learn that Lucy hated it when I was happy. I said to myself, "Maybe this was the key to life. Just be happy in all situations." I turned the car on, we buckled up, and drove to our appointment. When we got to the appointment, we checked in, and sat for roughly 10 minutes. A nursed called Lucy's name shortly after. I stayed seated and watched TV.

"Well, are you going to come with us or not?" Lucy asked.

"Oh I didn't know I was allowed to." I said sarcastically. I followed Lucy and the nurse to the room and sat down after the nurse closed the door. Lucy laid back on the bed and the nurse prepared her equipment to evaluate her.

"So, what are we doing today?" I asked the nurse.

"Listening to the heartbeat. She didn't tell you?"

"Yeah, I told him. He just wasn't listening." Lucy said. We both know Lucy never mentioned this, but I just played along. I ignored her comment and said, "Cool." When the nurse let us hear the heartbeat, I looked at Lucy and she was crying with tears of happiness. I looked at the nurse and said, "That is amazing." Even though I wasn't sure if the baby was mine or not, hearing that heartbeat made me feel warm inside. I smiled and looked at Lucy again.

"Why aren't you crying?" Lucy said with a demon tone in her voice…So I heard.

"Am I supposed to be?" I asked.

"WHY AREN'T YOU CRYING?" Lucy asked again.

"Lucy, just enjoy the moment for what it is." I said. She looked at the nurse, wiped the gel off her stomach, put her shirt on fully, and said, "We are done here." And began walking out of the room. I glanced at the nurse and we both had the look on our face like a deer staring into the headlights of a truck.

"My apologies for her behavior." I said to the nurse.

"It's ok. Can you just have her call to reschedule another appointment? She still needs to see the doctor." The nurse asked.

"Sure. I will relay that message to her." I said.

When I caught up to Lucy, she was standing by my car with her hands clinched together as if she wanted to fight me.

"Why the fuck weren't you crying? Do you even give a shit about this baby?" Lucy shouted. Before I replied, I looked at her in silence and thought to myself, "Damn…This woman really has a problem. Most people do not act like this. I hope whatever is making her behave this way can be resolved ASAP." Her attitude and mood swings were becoming harder to endure. The more I saw her like this, I began to look at her like a joke. At this point, she was a comedy show to me and I was just in the audience observing.

"People express emotions differently. And not everyone reacts the same way you do." I said as I looked at Lucy.

"You don't give a shit about me or the baby!" Lucy yelled and continue to curse me out until I dropped her off at her brothers. I ignored her and focused on the road, while thinking about eating my mother's food. When we got to her brother's house, Lucy exited my car immediately. I rolled my window down and said, "Lucy, you're wrong about one thing…I do give a shit about the baby. Oh, and the nurse wants you to reschedule another appointment when you get a chance." She looked at me, squinted her eyes like a baby tiger, grinded her teeth together, and walked backwards as she flipped me off with one middle finger. I smiled, waved back, and drove off bumping Serenade No. 13, "Eine Kleine Nachtmusik" in G Major by Mozart.

CHAPTER 11

BRUJA

One early morning, I was having breakfast with my mother. She cooked eggs, sausage, bacon, grits, and gravy, and toast with a side of strawberry jelly. I was on cloud 9 as I chewed every bite until I was interrupted by a phone call from Lucy. My phone vibrated because it was on silent.

Zrrr-Zrrr-Zrrr...

"Hello." I answered.

"I want you to meet my mom today." Lucy

said.

"Umm, ok? That is random but sure. We can do that. What time do you want to visit her?" I replied.

"In like ten minutes. My brother just dropped me off in front of your mom's house." Lucy said.

"Well, come inside. We are still eating breakfast. You are welcome to join us." I said. I dropped my fork, pushed my plate back, walked to the front door, opened it, and saw Lucy. She didn't say a word, pushed the door wide open, walked past me, and walked into the kitchen.

"Hi Lucy. Would you like something to eat?" My mother said.

"I don't eat that shit." Lucy replied.

My mother and I looked at her with a stunned facial expression.

"Excuse you. Do not be rude to my mother." I said as I looked at Lucy. She smiled and shrugged her shoulders.

"Are you almost done? My mother is expecting us." Lucy said. I sat down, finished my breakfast, washed my hands, and said, "Now, I am ready." I looked at my mother and shook my head in embarrassment. Lucy and I left, got into my car, and drove to her mother's house. Before we got there, we made a quick pit stop at the mall to get her mother a gift. When we arrived, we parked in the front of her house, I grabbed her mother's gift, and Lucy got out of my car immediately. Before we made it to the front door, Lucy's mother was standing outside, with her arms crossed, staring at us. She had blonde hair, dark circles under her eyes like Lucy. She wore a white shirt, blue jeans, and was wrapped in a white blanket. She looked like one of the ladies from an early 1990's movie called, "The Witches." Lucy's mother looked me up and down a few times, as I stood in front of her, holding her gift. Lucy walked past us and went inside to sit on the couch.

"Hi April. It is nice to finally meet you in person." I said as I handed her the gift. She grabbed it with two hands, stared at me and said, "Come in." I walked into the witches' den, and she closed the door behind me.

"You! Have a seat!" April said as she looked at me. I felt the tension immediately and went into defense mode.

"Say what?" I asked.

"Sit down now!" April said angrily.

"I'll stand. I'm good." I said in a serious manner. I looked at Lucy and said, "What is this?" Lucy started laughing and shrugged her shoulders. April changed her tone of voice, smiled, and asked, "Would you like to have a seat?"

"Sureeeeee." I replied in a sarcastic manner. I walked over to her couches and sat on the opposite end from Lucy.

"So, what do you want to be when you grow up?" April asked me.

"Huh?" I replied as I looked at both Lucy and April.

"WHAT DO YOU WANT TO BE WHEN YOU GROW UP?" April asked me again in a rude manner.

"I heard you. I just don't understand why you're asking me an absurd question." I replied.

"I am going to ask you again." April said. But before she could ask me her dumbass question, I cut her off and said, "And I'm going to tell you again." I looked at Lucy and said, "Are you going to let April talk to me like this?" Lucy smiled like the Grinch and began laughing like a dolphin. I got up and began walking towards the door.

"Mom, Justin is in the U.S. Navy and is currently in college. He plans to finish his bachelor's degree within the next few years." Lucy said.

"Wait, come back. I have a few more questions." April said in a jokingly manner. I stood at the front door and looked at both in silence. They looked like the cockroaches that were drinking coffee, from the movie, "Men in Black." They were laughing and staring at each other as if they were at a Kevin Hart's comedy show.

"I like that you have a career and goals. You have a good mindset. Please, come join us once again." April said. I was ready to go because I was already fed up with the nonsense and predicament, I was in. I also did not want to seem like a hot-headed douche bag or even let them get to me. So, I decided to turn around, sit down, and give them one more shot.

"So, what are your plans for this baby?" April asked.

"To love and support him or her. I also want Lucy to come back so we can work on this if it is mine." I replied.

"I don't want her to go back with you. I don't think it is a good idea." April said. I looked at Lucy, then back at April for a moment and said, "Well, that is not your choice. It's Lucy's."

"Well, if she was to go back with you, what about the car situation? Are you going to buy her a car?" April asked.

"I never said I was going to buy her a car. And plus, I already have one. She knows. She used it as if it was hers anyways. We can share my car if that is what you're asking." I replied.

"What about her bills and her college tuition. Are you going to take care of that?" April asked.

"What the heck are you talking

about?" I said with confusion. I knew April was trying to make me agree to promises that she wanted for her daughter. But I did not give in. Sure, I could take care of all these things, but it was not my duty or responsibility to give her a "free ride." My main objective was to take care of the baby if it was mine and "help" Lucy. Both were trying to take advantage of me because I was in the military.

"Well listen here, you are not good enough. She is too good for you. And plus, I don't like people like you." April said and she pointed at me up and down.

"What do you mean, people like me?" I asked.

"You know what I am talking about." April said.

"What, you don't like black people?" I asked. April smiled and started laughing.

"Yeah, people like YOU." April replied. I got up and announced, "I am done."

"Do you know how to train dogs?" April asked as I walked towards the door.

"What the hell?" I said as I looked at her. April called for one of her dogs, grabbed some treats, and I watched her pet it gently.

"Sit." April said as she held a treat over her dog's head. I was confused to what was going on. I should have left a long time ago, but I asked, "What is this about? I knew April was trying to change the subject and stall our conversation but why? I asked myself.

"Sometimes you just need to be more

like a dog and listen. But anyways, give me a hug." April said as she began to walk towards me with her arms wide open. I opened the door but before I could exit, she latched onto me. I stood there awkwardly until she released her filthy, witch hug. I stepped outside and looked back at both Lucy and April.

"It was nice meeting you." April said.

"Yeah...I wish I could say the same. Oh, and that apology text that I sent to you a while back...Lucy wrote it and she had me send it to you." I replied. I walked to my car feeling disoriented. When I took off, April and Lucy were standing outside watching me, as I looked in my rear-view mirror. "What the hell was that? Those witches are crazy. Now I see where Lucy gets it from." I said to myself. Later that night, I received a text from Lucy. She wrote, "Well, I guess everything went well. My mom kind of likes you...Just not for me though LOL." I didn't reply and just put my phone facing down on the counter.

CHAPTER 12

BALOONS IN A BOX

I was out one night with a few of my childhood friends, Darwin and Ana and received a text message from Lucy. She wrote, "We are doing a gender reveal at the beach tomorrow around 1:00 PM. You can come if you want." I wrote her back saying, "I will be there." After, I shrugged my shoulders and continued to laugh and play video games with Darwin and Ana. I felt like time stopped and all my worries faded away. From Lucy's actions to the way her mother treated me, I could care less about my encounters with them. My friends reminded me that, not everyone in the world is like them. And Lucy and her mother are just people that are not happy with their life. But regardless of how much fun I was having, I had to tell them about Lucy.

"So, do you guys remember seeing me with a blonde woman that was posted on my Instagram a while back?" I asked Darwin and Ana.

"Yeah. I also remember you telling us that she hacked your social media and was treating you like shit." Darwin said.

"Well, I fucked up. She may be pregnant. I am still waiting on the results but yeah…" I broke the news to them. Darwin and Ana looked at me but was not surprised.

"Dude, I felt like she was trying to trap you since the beginning because you're in the military. And from the looks of it, she did." Darwin said.

"Yeah, but all I can do is be there. So, having that said, we are doing a gender reveal at the beach. You guys are more than welcome to come." I mentioned. Darwin and Ana looked at each other and replied, "Yeah, we will be there." I gave them a hug and then went to visit my mom. It was roughly 11:00 PM and she was already in bed. I went into my old room, laid down, and thought to myself, "What the heck am I doing? Should I keep taking these punches from Lucy or should I just cut her off and wait until the paternity results come in? During that moment, I felt like taking the punches was my only option. I thought that I wanted her to come back, but hell no I was wrong. Which is why I still have not completed her last task. And that was to apologize to her in person. I knew she was waiting for me to do it. I know Lucy thought she had me by the balls, but I was just trying to feel her out. There was no way in hell would I ever live the rest of my life being abused by her.

The next day, I woke up, hit the beach, worked out near the water, grabbed breakfast, and got ready for the day. Lucy called me shortly after.

"Hey, I need you to take me to Walmart."
Lucy demanded.

"Do you mean, can I take you to
Walmart?" I replied. At this point, you
would think Lucy would know, that the little
feelings that I had for her has faded away
drastically. My attitude and demeanor
changed from being a "Slave to the game" to
being similar to Jamie Foxx in the movie
"Django." I was so over her shit, her racist
remarks, her racist mother, the way she
walked over me in the past, the way she
tried to manipulate every situation in her
favor, and most of all, the way she treated
me. Lucy wasn't used to me being serious or
correcting her.

"Uh yeah! That is what I said." Lucy replied
in an offensive manner.

"What time? And for what?" I asked.

"Like now and to get stuff for the gender
reveal." Lucy said. I drove over to her
brother's house, picked her up, and took her

to Walmart. We grabbed a few balloons and a large box. After, we headed over to my parents' house. My dad was feeling sick and just got home from the hospital. I gave both of my parent's hugs and hung out with them for a bit. Lucy went straight to my old room and didn't say a word.

"My dad asked, is that the evil girl your mama is talking about?

"Yes. We are doing a gender reveal and she is getting the stuff together." I replied. Both of my parents looked at each other and smirked.

"Justin! I need you to put this damn box together." Lucy shouted. I looked at my parents and said with embarrassment, "I'll be right back." As I was putting the box together, Lucy kept staring at me.

"Do you even know what you are doing? You are not handy at all. How long is this going to take?" Lucy mumbled under her breath.

141

"Do you want to put this together?" I asked. Lucy just gawked at me like a sloth in silence. It took me a total of ten minutes to fix her box the way she wanted it. Lucy grabbed the box, threw the pack of balloons inside, and walked out the back door.

"Where are you going?" I asked.

"To the beach. My friend is outside with her truck, and I am going to put this in the back of it. Invite your parents, invite your friends, and I will meet you there." Lucy said. I watched her leave and then I got ready. I told my parents about the gender reveal event and my mother said they cannot make it because my dad was too sick to stand up. I gave both hugs and left. When I got to the beach, I saw Lucy with her friends and family. Lucy walked up to me and said, "Where is your parents? The only people that showed up was Darwin and Ana."

"Well, my dad is too sick to stand up." I replied. Lucy looked at me like she wanted to tear my head off.

"Why didn't you tell anyone else?" Lucy asked.

"Let's enjoy this." I said as I proceeded to walk to the gender reveal site. Lucy sped past me and joined her friends and family.

"Hey Justin!" Darwin said.

"Hey guys. Thank you for coming. This should be quick." I replied.

"No worries." Darwin said. As I joined Lucy on the beach, in front of the box, she yelled, "Ok, is everyone ready?" And a few took out their phones to grab pictures and videos.

"10...9...8...7...6...5...4...3...2...1..." Everyone counted down. We opened the box, and the balloons were released into the sky. I looked up and saw pink balloons. "It's a girl! The crowd shouted." I looked over at Lucy and she was smiling. I gave her a hug and said, "Well, right on! It's a girl." Lucy's mother came up to me with opened arms and said, "Bring it in." I hesitated for a moment and then gave her a side hug. Shortly after, everyone scattered and began walking towards their cars. Lucy already took off and was walking with her friends. I caught up to her and said, "Hey, would you like to get a bite to eat?"

"Get the fuck away from me. What do you think this is?" Lucy said quietly so her friends wouldn't hear her.

"Alright. I have shit to do anyways." I said. I received a text from my ex-wife, and she told me that my daughter Ashley just got back from Utah. She was out there for a softball tournament and now they are back in town. So, I left and went to pick her up. I took her out to eat, and then we went to my parents' house. 30 minutes later, Lucy showed up unexpectedly.

"What are you doing here?" I asked.

"We need to get my dad and brothers the gifts you promised at the mall. We are having dinner with them." Lucy said.

"Dude, you can't just show up and expect me to cater to you. And plus, I am with Ashley right now." I replied in a serious manner. Ashley walked up and overheard what we were talking about and said, "I want to go to the mall."

"See, she wants to go. Let's go to the mall now." Lucy demanded. I shook my head, and we left my parents' house. When we got to the mall, I told Ashley that she could get whatever she wanted. So, she walked to the toys section and began looking. Lucy left my side, grabbed a cart, and began loading it with random items. She made a few trips around the whole store. When she got back to Ashley and me, the cart that she had was filled to the top.

"Daddy, can I have this?" Ashley asked and held up a little monster high doll.

145

"Put that shit back! This trip isn't for you."
Lucy shouted at Ashley.

"Hey what's the deal? Why are you
shouting at her? And what is all this stuff?" I
asked.

"It's all on sale. It shouldn't be that much."
Lucy said. I looked at her and began
walking towards the checkout line. I told
Ashley to grab the monster high doll and
come with me. I paid for Ashley's doll and
gave it to her. She hugged it and said,
"Thank you daddy!" Lucy began loading all
her items and when she was done, the
cashier said, "That will be, $1246.69."

"So, Lucy, this doesn't look like the items
you had back in New York. And it was for
sure not, $1246.69 worth." I said. Lucy
shrugged her shoulders and said, "Well, I
don't have the money. I thought you were
going to pay for this stuff." I looked at the
cashier and the long ass line behind me. I
heard people mumbling things under their
breath in an annoyed manner.

146

"So, will you be paying with cash or card?" The cashier asked me. I hesitated for a moment and just wanted to leave the store. So, I took my card out and said, "Card…" I put it into the reader, entered my pin, waited for the beep, and took my card out once the transaction when through. After we left the store, we went back to my parent's house and began wrapping the gifts.

"We need to hurry up. My dad is waiting for us, and he is cooking a big dinner tonight." Lucy said.

"Say what? I didn't know this was all happening tonight. I won't be able to make it. And plus, I still have Ashley with me." I replied.

"Well, I don't have a ride." Lucy said. I took a deep breath in, looked at Ashley, and exhaled. The only thing that I wanted to do was spend time with Ashley alone. And having Lucy around was making it extra difficult. So, I made a choice to drop Ashley

off, pick her up tomorrow, and take Lucy to
visit her dad hoping she would stay there for
the rest of the time. When we arrived in San
Diego at her dad's house, we parked in front
of his driveway. He was standing outside
watering the grass at night. I thought that
was kind of odd but just went with it. He
had dark brown hair with a little gray in it,
he wore tiny glasses with a silver frame, a
black faded t-shirt, jean shorts, and sandals.
Lucy and I got out of the car, she went up to
him, and he gave her a big hug. I watched
him squeeze her tight, as his hands went
down to her butt. He gave a little smack,
looked at her breast, and made a comment
about them. I remember Lucy told me he
was a pervert, but I didn't believe it until I
witness this moment. When he saw me, he
smiled and said, "Hey Justin!" As he
reached out with his right hand. "Nice to
meet you, Bret." I said as I shook his hand.
Before letting my hand go, he brought me in
for a hug. Bret smelled like 5 shots of
tequila. Other than that, he was a nice guy
and was far different from Lucy's mother.

"Whatever Lucy said about you, I don't see it." Bret said. I looked at him with confusion and followed them into his house.

"I cooked a lot of food. I hope you guys are hungry." Bret said as he uncovered the food like a magician. Lucy's brothers were sitting on the couch and said, "Hey guys." I waved at them, walked over, and shook their hands.

"Hey B.J., Do you remember that apology text message I sent you a while back?" I asked.

"Yeah…" B.J. replied.

"Lucy wrote it and had me send it to you." I said and smiled and walked away. I thought to myself, "Mission accomplished. The truth is set free. I told Lucy's mom and her brother who really sent that awful text. But wait, why am I even happy about this? What mission did I accomplish? Even though the truth is out, who are they going to believe?" I looked at B.J. and he stared at the ground with an odd facial expression as if he ate something sour.

"Before we eat, let's take a shot of tequila." Bret said as he poured everyone, except Lucy a glass. "I usually don't drink liquor." I mentioned. His smile turned into a frown immediately. I paused and said, "But tonight, I'll have one." He shouted, "Hell yeah!" And handed me a shot. Everyone held their glasses in the air and Bret said, "A toast to all of you." And through the drink back with ease. He poured me another and said, "Welcome to the family." I felt awkward, smiled, and drank the second shot.

"So, have you met April yet?" Bret asked.

"Yeah he met mom." Lucy replied.

"And how did that go?" He asked.

"It was interesting." I said.

"I must say, she is different." Bret

150

said as he looked at the ground. We chatted for a while and at the end of our conversation, Bret said, "Welcome to the family once again. I really like you. And whatever Lucy said about you, I definitely do not believe it."

"Well, since you mentioned that twice, what did she say about me?" I asked as I looked at Lucy.
"Stop! Let's talk about something else." Lucy said.

"I will be right back; I have to get you guys something." I said, as I excused myself and went to my car. Lucy and I almost forgot to give them the gifts that we wrapped. I brought them in the house and handed everyone their gifts. Lucy's dad loved the candles we bought him. He talked about them for hours and then showed me how he liked to trim the tips before lighting it. We ended up having a good time and I thought her dad was a great guy. Lucy on the other hand looked like she hated that I got along with her family. On the way home she said,

"See, I told you my dad would like you. And he is probably the only one." I didn't respond. When we got back to my parent's house, Lucy started complaining about random things. I felt like she was trying to start an argument for no reason.

"These sheets are too warm. You are dumb. You know, my dad may like you, but my brothers don't." Lucy said.

"Its Christmas Eve. We had a great night and let's leave it like that. If you truly have an issue with me, let's talk about it on the 26th of December. Let's enjoy this." I said. She continued to get louder and curse me out for no reason.

"You want me to go back to New York with you, right?" Lucy asked.

"I wanted you to come back." I replied.

"Well, apologize to me. And do it on your fucking knee's." Lucy said.

152

"Oh...So, that's why you wanted me to apologize to you in person. Makes sense..." I said in a comically manner.

"Get on your fucking knee's now!" Lucy demanded.

I laughed, walked away, and decided to go into a different bedroom to lay down. Moments later, I heard the front door shut and saw Lucy loading her luggage into a white car. I laid back down with a smile on my face and slept like a baby.

CHAPTER 13

JUNE 9, 2018

After Christmas break, I went back to New York and felt something in my apartment, that I haven't in a long time. "Serenity and peace." I felt like I wanted to do more, go out, explore, and make this duty station a wonderful experience for me. Without having Lucy around, my stress levels decreased significantly. I felt a bit traumatized before leaving New York to enjoy my Christmas break. I learned that I cannot let someone else control my life. I learned that people are going to be the way they want, and it is not my duty to change that. Even if it's for the better. Some people are kind, and some are not. I also learned that I cannot let someone else's behavior be the foundation to how I feel about others.

Before Christmas break, I would look in the mirror and say to myself, "I am done with "dating" for a long time… I don't need anyone else…Being alone is so much better." But in reality, I did not mean that. After weeks of conducting the same "boring" routine, I decided to be spontaneous. I started going out alone. I went to the movies, played pool, hiked, and went out for dinner. One night, I was out at the local bar after work. I saw a couple of guys I knew from my unit playing pool. They noticed me and asked if I wanted to play a few games. I walked over to them, gave them a dap, and said, "Hell yeah. I am down." The guys and I played for a few hours and in the middle of it, I stopped to grab a few beers for them. As I was waiting for the bartender to order a few drinks, a woman gently bumped into me and said in a weird accent, "Hey. Sorry about that. I dropped my paper."

"Hi. And no worries…Your accent is cool. Where are you from?" I said.

"I am from New Jersey." She replied.

"Nice. What's your name?" I asked.

"Rachele."

"Awesome." I said, as I looked passed her noticing that she had three of her girlfriends with her. There was one that caught my attention. I tried not to get caught looking at her, but she saw me. This woman had, long slick black hair, red lipstick, a black dress on, a pearl necklace, red heels, and a nice tan with a well-built frame. She looked like she was a gymnast/tennis player in her past life.

"Hey, I know you. I've seen you before." The woman behind Rachele said.

"Where have you seen me?" I asked.

"You are my neighbor. You live right down the street from me. Not to be creepy, but I saw you running a few times." She said.

"That is not creepy. I do run a lot and plus, this is a small town. What is your name by the way?" I said.

"Arelia. And these other girls are Melissa and Jackie. And you already met Rachele I see." She said. We chatted for a bit, I got Arelia's number, and went back to hang out with my boys.

"Hey dude. I thought you were grabbing us beers?" One of the guys named Buzz asked.

"My bad man. I got a little distracted by a few ladies." I said as I pointed at the bar. But then, I noticed that Arelia and her friends already left.

"What ladies?" Buzz asked.

"They were just there." I said. As I looked with confusion. I said, "Oh, well. Maybe they are ninjas." And walked back to the bar and got my buddies the beers I didn't get the first time. After another game, I decided to call it a night and went home. The next morning, I texted Arelia and asked her if she wanted to hangout. She agreed and overtime, we became great friends. We spent a lot of time together. She was the friend that I never had. Arelia didn't judge me, was kind, smart, and made me want to become more of myself. She never made me feel less of a human. Whenever I felt down, she would always lift me up. And she said that I did the same thing for her. I liked how everything felt natural when we were together. This was the first time I felt like someone didn't want something from me except my time. After months of "hanging out" we decided to become a couple. But before we made it official, I told her about Lucy and what I was going through. And she said, "I will have your back no matter what." This gave me strength. I learned that I no longer must fight this battle alone but at the same time, I won't ever get Arelia involved with my situation physically. She was my support system mentally and is still till this day.

One day, I received a text from Lucy. She asked, "Can I have a few hundred dollars? I need some groceries." And sent me a picture of her empty fridge. I looked at the picture, thought of the baby, and felt bad. I texted her back immediately and said, "Yeah. I got you. Do you want me to send it to your Venmo?"

"Yes. And can you also order me a Pizza in the meantime?" Lucy asked. I agreed and made things happen. Minutes later, I went on Amazon and ordered baby clothes, toys, food, formula, and diapers. I sent it to Lucy with the fastest delivery time. I didn't tell her. And I just continued to do this for months. Each paycheck, on the first and the fifteenth, I would get a text from Lucy. And she would request hundreds of dollars. During that time, and even though I was still waiting on the paternity test results, I thought it was only right to continue giving Lucy what she needed. Then finally, I received a call from Lucy saying, "Are you the one ordering all of this baby stuff?" I said, "Yes."

"Well, the baby might be born in Late June. You can come if you want." Lucy said.

"I am scheduled to be out at sea during that timeframe, but I will do my best to make it. Just let me know an approximate date. I need to request leave time." I replied. After I sent that, I did not hear back from Lucy for months. As June was approaching, I continued to text and call Lucy to see if she had an estimated date. But she kept ignoring my calls and messages. I requested leave for the end of June, but my Commander did not approve it.

"We will be at sea. And this time of the year, it is important for you to be with us." My Commander said. I told her about my situation, and she stated that I needed to give her more details with an exact date. She also reminded me that I must always know that the mission comes first. It was impossible at this point because I couldn't get a hold of Lucy. So, I went on my mission. Out at sea, I barely had any service. But once we reached certain ports, I was able to get minor reception. On an early morning, my unit and I pulled into a port located at Ft. Lauderdale, Florida.

"Zrrr…Zrrr…Zrrr…"

My phone was vibrating because the signal was decent. A ton of messages and a few missed calls flooded my notification bar. I noticed that a few of the text messages were from Lucy. So, I opened hers. One message said, "Are you coming?" Another message read, "Here is a picture of Nina." I called her a few times, but she didn't pick up. So, I texted her.

"Nina…Great name. When can I meet her?" I didn't receive a text back for a month. On the second day of July, my phone was going off. I took it out of my right pocket and saw it was Lucy.

"YOU WERE SUPPOSED TO BE HERE. WHY AREN'T YOU HERE?" Lucy shouted.

161

"I told you that I needed to know an approximate date in advance. I can't just ask my unit to take me home because you texted me. So, when can I meet Nina?" I replied. Lucy hung up. I tried to call her back, but she declined my call. I decided to give her a few days to cool off and then I called her again. Lucy sent me straight to voicemail yet again. This went off for weeks until I stopped calling. Even though the paternity results still haven't come in yet, I felt bad because part of me wanted to be there. Later that night, I was hanging out with Arelia.

"Are you ok? You haven't been yourself lately." Arelia asked.

"I have been trying to get a hold of Lucy to schedule sometime to meet the baby, but she continues to ignore my calls." I replied.

"You are not even sure if the baby is yours or not. Worry about that when the time comes." Arelia said. I looked at the ground, stared at the ants carrying an injured one. I noticed that, even the smallest among us who love one another, never leave a fallen comrade.

I felt like the injured ant and Arelia was the one carrying me. And she wasn't going to leave me hanging by any means. I felt this way because if the tables were turned, I would do the same thing for her. She's a person that sets my soul on fire and brings me back to life. Especially at my lowest points.

"Anyways...Your birthday is coming up and I got us something special." Arelia said.

"Oh yeah? And what's that?" I asked.

"Tickets to Bali! You just have to book the hotels. Are you down for that?" She asked.

"What? That's insane! And hell yeah I am down for that." I said with excitement and gave her a hug.

"Great. Worry less and enjoy your special day." Arelia said. She always amazed me and helped me keep my mindset right. We ended up spending 5 days in Bali. Arelia and I had the best time ever. We hung out in our bungalow that floated over the water, did yoga every morning, and ate food that was to die for. I felt like time stopped while we were there. And when we got back, I was refreshed and ready to take on any task…Well it sure felt like that until the second week. One day, when I got off work, I was greeted by a Sheriff at my front door.

"Are you Justin Blane?" The Sheriff asked.

"Yes. How can I help you?" I asked.

"This is for you." The Sheriff said and handed me a brown envelope.

"Thank you, sir. I appreciate it." I said and walked into my front door. "Court orders from Lucy. What's this? Lucy is requesting backpay and child support? Great…" I said to myself.

Lucy managed high end condos in La Costa, CA which ran for roughly $3700 a month. She was paid good money to do it without a license. She also rented a condo on the same property. A few days later, I went to court and was told to bring in all my sources of income. I only had one because being in the U.S. Navy was my only job. After letting the judge review my paperwork and Lucy's, he finalized an arrangement. Lucy was awarded to received $811 a month and $6000 worth of backpay. When I reviewed the paperwork, I noticed that Lucy wrote down that she only made $600 a month. I thought to myself, "How is that even possible if she lives in a $3700 condo? Are the courts blind? Is the system broken? When was this child support system last updated?" I had many questions. I wasn't worried about making the payments. I was just worried that Lucy would spend all of the baby's money on herself.

A few months later, I was attending a military school that lasted about a few months. Through that time, I barely had service yet again. When I did, I would check my messages and social media from time to time. One month in, I remember logging into Instagram, and I saw that Lucy tagged me in a photo. It was a picture of a ghost pushing a stroller. The caption read, "Look, I am Nina's father for Halloween." A joke that she stole from her brother. I didn't pay any attention to it but before I exited her page, I saw a picture of my cousin commenting under her caption. He wrote, "Yeah. I can't believe that fool! And agreeing with other negative comments. I could care less about what people say but when its my own family, I immediately felt disappointed. I took a screenshot of her post, created a family group text, included my cousin, and sent the screenshot of Lucy's post. I wrote, "I am not mad at you. I am just disappointed. My cousin immediately wrote back and said, "I was just trying to help."

"You don't even know half of the story. You don't know what I am going through with this woman. But again, I am not mad at you. I am just disappointed." I wrote.

"I was just trying to help. I am not trying to get on your bad side because no one likes that...I was just trying to help." My cousin wrote. I sat on my bunk, stared at my phone, and thought, "How was he trying to help? Does he know that Lucy's racist? Does he know that she slapped and abused me multiple times? Does he know that it was her magnificent obsession to try and trap me?" I answered my own questions for him. "No..." In fact, I didn't even know they were friends on Instagram.

CHAPTER 14

MEETING NINA

After I graduated from the military course I was attending, I took leave and caught a flight to California. Once I landed, I met up with my family. Including my cousin Jaydee who disappointed me with his comments on Lucy's "Ghost pushing a stroller" post on Instagram. Jaydee and I had a casual conversation. I didn't look at him any different, but I did fill him in on what I was going through with Lucy.

"Damn fool. I didn't know "ALL THAT."
Jaydee said with a dumbfounded look on his
face.

"Yeah...And I am still waiting on the
paternity test results." I said.

"I believe you Justin but...She doesn't look
like the type to..." Jaydee said as my phone
rang.

"Speaking of the devil. Look who is
calling me...Lucy! I'll put it on speaker and
let you get a taste of the real her." I said to
Jaydee as I showed him my phone. He
looked at me, gave me a nod, I pressed the
green accept button, and took Lucy's call.

"Hello." I answered.

"When the fuck are you going to
meet Nina?" Lucy said as I looked at
Jaydee, like the shrunken head, at the end of
Beetlejuice. His jaw dropped and his
eyebrows rose like the McDonald's arches.

"Well actually...I am in Oceanside right now. How about I stop by your house today?" I asked.

"What? You didn't tell me you were fuckin' coming." Lucy said irritably.

"Was I supposed to?" I chuckled.

"Yeah. Everything is a joke to you...I don't want your fuckin' ass to come over to my house. I will drive over to you." Lucy said.

"Sounds good. I am staying at my mom's house. 12:00 PM would be a great time to swing by." I said.

"You don't tell me what time to bring her you bitch. I will be there at 12:30 PM." Lucy said and hung up. She had a habit of never agreeing with me. But I didn't mind because I knew her presence in my life, from there on out, would only be temporary.

"What in the world was that?" Jaydee asked as he stared at me uncomprehendingly.

"Now that...That was nothing. Wait until you see her in person. She's a bit different." I said. The next day, Lucy showed up to my mom's house at 12:45 PM. My mother and Jaydee were in the kitchen hanging out.

"Hi Lucy. Please, come in." I said with a smile on my face.

"Thirty minutes." Lucy said.

"Thirty minutes?" I asked.

"You get thirty minutes with her." Lucy said as she held and pointed at Nina.

"Hi Nina. Nice to meet you." I said as I shook Nina's little hand.

"Do you want to hold her?" Lucy said angrily.

171

"Of course, I want to." I replied as Lucy put Nina on the ground.

"If she doesn't know you, she won't come up to you. Just saying." Lucy said. Nina paused for a second and immediately crawled over to me. She put her hands up as if she wanted me to elevate her life. I picked her up gently and brought her closer to my heart.

"Be careful!" Lucy shouted. My mother and I looked at each other with such bewilderment but proceeded to shift our focus on Nina shortly after. Lucy hovered over Nina and I as we were interacting with each other. She kept a short distance between us and did not give us space to breathe. I caught her snapping a few pictures of us when she thought I wasn't looking. I said, "Here, I will pose for you." And Lucy snapped a few more pictures embarrassingly.

"Would you mind if I spend a few hours with her?" I asked.

"Hell yeah I would mind. I don't trust you with her! Give her back." Lucy said as she reached over to grab Nina. Lucy was at my mother's house for a total of 20 minutes. And began walking towards the front door promptly.

"We have to go! But if you want to see her again, just stop by my house tomorrow at 12:00 PM." Lucy said as she left.

"Weird right?" I said to Jaydee.

"Yeah…Pretty weird." Jaydee replied.

"Do you and Xena want to come with me to visit Nina tomorrow? I asked. Xena is my cousin's wife.

Yeah. We can go. I'll tell her." Jaydee said.
The next day, Jaydee, Xena, and I got in my car and drove to Lucy's house. I texted, "On my way!" And Lucy read my text without replying. When we arrived, Jaydee and Xena

173

were standing on the left side of the door, and I was in front of it. When I knocked on Lucy's door, she thought I was alone because she did not see Jaydee and Xena.

"You got 30 minutes mother fucker. You hear me?" Lucy said in a demon voice. I paused, smiled, and looked over at Jaydee and Xena.

"Well guys, it looks like we only have 30 minutes." I said in a sarcastic manner and stared at Lucy. She stuck her head out of her door, paused with embarrassment, gave Jaydee and Xena a fake smile, and said, "Come in! Hurry up!" As she waved us in, looked both ways, and shut her door.

"Do you want to feed her?" Lucy asked.

"Of course." I replied. Lucy handed me a baby spoon and baby food. I walked over to Nina and began feeding her as she smiled at me the whole time. When we got to the last scoop of food, Lucy snatched the spoon from me and said, "Ok! That's it. She is tired! You guys need to leave." And hurried us out of her house. Jaydee, Xena, and I walked back to my car and left immediately. As we were on our way home, I fixed my rearview mirror and focused it on Jaydee. He instantly locked eyes with me. I asked, "So, if I was to share this story in court, who are they going to believe?"

CHAPTER 15

THE UNWANTED GUEST

After a few months of being back in New York, I was told that Lucy has been hanging out with my family members and personally inviting them to events. I wasn't surprised. Lucy knew how much family meant to me and she was willing to do whatever it took to get my attention. I didn't like what she was doing because I wasn't even sure if Nina was my child or not. I also found it odd that she wanted to hang out with my family all the sudden.

Beep…Beep…Beep. My phone rang.

"Hey what's up bro?" I answered.

"Hey man. I went to Lucy's baby shower and her neighbor was speaking highly of you. He really likes you man. And dude…She has been telling us stories about you two, but I find them hard to believe." My brother Jason said.

"What stories?" I asked.

"She said you destroyed her gifts that she bought with her hard-earned money and how you kicked her out of your apartment." Jason said.

"Ha-ha-ha!" I laughed. "My apologies bro but, did she tell you how I just took off the wrapping paper on the gifts and she's started chucking them at me? Did she tell you that I gave her $300, and she went on a $1000 plus spending spree in December with my card to replace those items? Did she tell you…" I stopped myself mid-sentence and looked at the wall. I thought to myself, "Why am I explaining all of this?"

"No. She didn't mention any of that...Listen, I don't know the full story but bro, I got your back. I know this is a tough situation but just keep pushing through. Fight for what you believe in." Jason said.

"Right now, you don't know the full story but one day, you will." I replied. Lucy was into the business of "Trying" to convince others that she is this perfect angel. When she was with me, I said to myself, "First, she shared stories of how broke she was. I didn't buy it because I knew she grew up in a high-class neighborhood. Second, she shared stories of how her mother used to leave her alone for days at a time. She said her mother would rather spend time with her flight instructor, who later became her boyfriend, and presently, her husband. Lucy

178

said that she would starve and just eat spoons full of sugar to survive. I kind of bought that story. Third, Lucy shared disturbing stories of her family members. Now those stories…I bought." But what was she up to with mine?" I pondered.

"I think she thought we would just take her word for it and automatically hate you." Jason said.

"That's it! That's fuckin' it! Bro, she was trying to hit me where my heart is. What a savage." I said.

"Yeah, that girl is ruthless. But that's not how us Blane's roll." Jason said. I smiled and we ended up chatting about exciting topics for several minutes. After hanging up with Jason, my ex-wife, Mary called.

"I agree with Lucy. The girls should meet

179

each other." Mary said.

"What the heck are you talking about?" I asked.

"Lucy didn't tell you? She said that you were cool with the girls meeting each other next week." Mary said.

"I never said anything like that. And didn't know you guys were friends. Do you guys speak often?" I said in a sarcastic manner.

"Yes. Ashley and Nina FaceTime, a lot. Speaking of Ashley...Say high to your daddy." Mary said as she passed the phone to Ashley.

"Hi Ashley." I said.

"Hi daddy." Ashley replied gently. I

asked her how she was doing and chatted for a few minutes about life. Before she gave the phone back to Mary, I asked her if she talked to Lucy. And Ashley said, "Yes. She is very scary. She forces me to talk to Nina and she stares at me like a witch. She's scary daddy. I don't like speaking to her on FaceTime."

"It's ok Ashley. I will take care of this." I said as she handed the phone back to Mary. "Let me be the one to bring the girls together. My situation has nothing to do with you." I said.

"Well now it does." Mary said and hung up. I took a deep breath and exhaled. I looked at my phone for a few seconds and decided to call Lucy. I was full of rage because she was destroying my personal relationships that did not have anything to do with her. She was invading my family territory. She was trying to cause storms in places that she didn't have any business being in. And this was all because I did not feel the same way she did about me.

"Hello." Lucy answered.

"Do not hang out with my family when I am not present. And stop contacting my daughter Ashley." I said.

"Bitch! Who the fuck do you think you are? Do you think you can just call me and demand I do things for you?" Lucy asked.

"Do not hang out with my family when I am not present. And stop contacting my daughter Ashley." I repeated and hung up. A few days later, my mother called and told me that Lucy randomly showed up to her house with Nina and has been doing this each week since I left. She also said that

Lucy gave her a picture of Nina and demanded that she hung it up immediately.

"Mom, I am sorry that this is happening. I will bring it up in court next week." I said. My mother and I talked for thirty minutes about other things and then wished me luck in court. Fast forwarding to my court date with Lucy, everything lasted roughly 20 minutes. Since I was in New York, and Lucy was in California, we had a teleconference court session. A lot of irrelevant topics were brought up on Lucy's end. One that stood out was my Instagram. Lucy took screen shots of my Bali trip with Arelia, printed them, and shared it in court. She said that I had a lot of money and spent most of it on vacation. The judge did not care about any of that. He said, "Mr. Blane can spend his money any way he likes. What I care about is how he is going to take care of Nina." The judge said the paternity test result came back and I was the father. I was not disappointed because I have been prepared. I asked for full custody and I was denied because I was in the military. Days went by and when I try to set a schedule to see Nina, Lucy would curse me out and try to make this process harder. Lucy went out of her way to put a restraining order on me because she "heard" I was going to do that to her. Although she slapped me around a few times, I didn't file a restraining order. Lucy would block my calls often and went out of her way to change her number. I didn't chase or bother to play her game because I was not interested. I know she was satisfied because she was getting a huge chunk of my military paycheck and she "thought" she had me in a "checkmate" status. But I couldn't have been because she was playing this game alone. I continued to send messages to Lucy about spending time with Nina but stopped when I had enough. I had to approach things differently. Instead of running around in circles with Lucy, the California Court System, and getting nowhere, I decided to write you this book. This book is for my family members and the rest of the world because you have not heard my story. I felt like I have grown and took on a whole new mindset. This situation showed me that its ok to ask for help but it's not ok to remain silent. My voice and all those victims that are in a similar situation matter. It took me a long time to tell anyone my story because it lingered in the depths of my heart. For once in my life, I felt hopeless, and I wanted to quit. I felt like I was a "punk" because I was abused by a "White, blonde, woman. I felt like talking about this situation would make me be less of a man. But no! Those feelings were all wrong. I now feel free and relieved that I no longer must hide in the shadows. There are many stories out there but there is only one

of mine. The truth. But…Who are you going
to believe?

CHAPTER 16

LETTER TO NINA

On an early morning, I thought to myself, "When Nina is old enough to understand these true events, I want her to know the side she was never told." I know the language within this book can at times be very explicit, but don't mind me. I did that on purpose. If you haven't read or heard a curse word yet trust me, you will. If you made it to chapter 16, congratulations! You read or heard most of them. But back to Nina, I want her to know that I do not have a filter when it comes to the truth. To end on a comforting note, this letter is for her...

Dear Nina,

I got love for you. I met you only a
few times, but I hope we can have more.
Right now, I know you are too young to
understand but one day I hope this book will
answer most of your questions. Just know
that I've always wanted to, and still want to
be there for you. If your mom ever has a
change of heart or if the California court
systems shall work in my favor, we are
going to have the best time ever. I am a fun
guy and I love anything that keeps me
active. I love laughing and sharing funny
stories. I am a spaghetti lover and I hope we
can enjoy a huge plate together. I've had
visions of us watching movies, going out to
play miniature golf, and fishing together.
I've dreamt of us falling asleep as we laid in
a hammock near the beach. Aside from my
visions and dreams, I just want to let you
know that you have your whole life ahead of
you and great things will come your way if

188

you keep an open heart. And what I mean by that is, love others as much as you love yourself. You are the creator of your own reality. Anything that you want, you can have. And anything that you can imagine, you can create physically. I am telling you these things because some of us tend to forget. And I don't want that to happen to you.

Anyways, I know I am a stranger to you, and you are to me, but the love that I feel, eliminates that feeling. You might not know this, but you are my inspiration. You inspired me to write this book. I have kept all of this to myself, minus a handful of people. But you gave me the courage to stand up. I used to keep everything to myself and not say a word if anything negative would happen to me. Especially if it made me feel less of a "Macho Man." So, I want to say, "Thank you for giving me strength. There are many stories floating around but there is only one of mine. I kept my silence for so long because I did not know how to approach this situation without feeling a mixture of emotions. I felt like I didn't have the courage to fight for the first time in my life. I felt like I didn't have the money or resources to back me up. I felt like I didn't have the right people in my corner. I felt like I didn't have the right mindset. I broke down many times and I almost gave up. But there was one thing on my mind that did not allow me to quit. And that was you...Thank you for being here on this planet.

Love,

Me

MEET THE AUTHOR

Raynaldo "Ray" Cruz Duffy, grew up in the sunny city of Oceanside, California. He enlisted in the U.S. Army a little after high school and served two tours in Iraq. A graduate with a degree in business and another in Military Leadership, he has contributed to helping others enhance their lives. Duffy is a Military Personnel & Administrative Specialist for the Department of Defense and writes children's books in his spare time. Duffy lives in Martinsburg, West Virginia with his wife, son, dog and two rabbits.

Made in the USA
Las Vegas, NV
20 April 2022

47717066R00115